Arts Integration
Ideas for the Dynamic Classroom Teacher

Daryl R. Worley ■ **Jodie H. Schenck**

Texas A & M University Commerce

Kendall Hunt
publishing company

About the Pearce Museum At Navarro College:

From the war-weary letter, Colonel Joshua Chamberlain wrote to his wife from the Antietam battlefield, to Howard Terpning's artistic interpretation of a Native American grandfather sharing wisdom with his grandchildren, and an archaeological survey of stone tools from the Blackland Prairie of Texas; The Pearce Museum At Navarro College's unique collections give visitors and researchers a chance to consider the unthinkable sacrifices of the American soul, ponder the transformation of the American conscience during the last half of the nineteenth century and beyond, and appreciate how prehistoric hunter-gatherers lived in our local area.

Our museum consists of our Civil War Collection, comprising of over 15,000 letters and diaries. We have sought to include perspectives from all people involved in the war—North and South, men and women, children and adults, leaders and common citizens. The museum's Western Art Collection contains a vast variety of medias from Contemporary artists, which depict either the historic or modern American West. The Hunter Gatherers From The Blackland Prarie Exhibit provides an interactive learning experience, teaching visitors about our prehistoric heritage.
Staff and volunteers are dedicated to the visitor experience and committed to excellence in every aspect of the preservation of our collections, and our educational programs that serve the public.

Please visit us at www.pearcemuseum.com for more information about our hours, tours, and programs.

Citation: Terpning, Howard. *Grandfather Speaks*. 2002. Oil on canvas, 40 × 44 in. The Pearce Museum At Navarro College, Corsicana Texas.

Kendall Hunt
publishing company

www.kendallhunt.com
Send all inquiries to:
4050 Westmark Drive
Dubuque, IA 52004-1840

CONTENTS

ABOUT THE AUTHORS

Daryl R. Worley A native Texan with a New Mexican influence. Born close to Amarillo, but raised in Clovis, New Mexico, Daryl was exposed to a variety of Artistic experiences in the classroom and the community. He holds a BSE from Howard Payne University where he majored in Education, Studio Art and Theatre with a minor in music. After teaching high school theatre for nearly 10 years, he entered the world of professional theatre as a director and producer of plays and musicals. Daryl graduated from Baylor University in 2006 with his Master of Arts degree in directing and began teaching at the college level and writing and directing plays. Daryl has taught theatre for Navarro College for 10 years and Texas A & M University Commerce for five years. His published works include *Theatre Through the Ages: An Introduction to Theatre* as well as a cookbook and numerous professional journal articles. Daryl is presently a doctoral candidate, studying curriculum and instruction at Liberty University in Lynchburg, Virginia. Daryl resides in Texas with his wife Christa and son Greerson.

Jodie H. Schenck A Texas artist with a BFA from Stephen F. Austin University, trained in studio art and art history as well as a Masters of Education from Texas Women's University, Jodie is a passionate artist. Serving for over 27 years in the classroom Jodie continues to develop teaching methods that serve college students as well as junior high students. With a variety of teaching experience including, developing an art curriculum for a small private school, working with reluctant students seeking a GED including incarcerated students seeking an education and developing the minds of young junior high students who pass through the door of her classroom. In addition to teaching junior high students Jodie has taught developmental classes for a junior college and teaches future teachers at Texas A & M University Commerce. Jodie is hard at work writing a new book, *Teaching Icons I Have Known*. She resides in Texas with her husband Dave.

FORWARD

Throughout this book, you will find stories as examples demonstrating the dynamic effect that lessons with elements of art, music, or theatre have on students in the classroom. The arts have the power to change lives and create lasting memories in the classroom. The following pages are a brief glimpse of some of these possibilities within a classroom.

ACKNOWLEDGMENT

This book is dedicated to Sheila Herod and Sheryl Young, two special teachers who encouraged and helped the authors in writing this book.

CHAPTER I
Art Is Expression

Human beings were created to communicate and express themselves. Expression has taken many forms and evolved into a variety of forms since Adam and Eve first explored the apple. Consider early man going out for the hunt to bring back food for their families in the cave. After a long-day chasing, buffalo imagine the men sitting around a campfire exchanging hunting stories. As the stories progress, one man jumps up and begins to act out the actual events related to hunting the buffalo. Another man jumps up and begins to draw a picture on the cave wall showing the buffalo and several men with spears hunting. Meanwhile another man jumps up and takes two dried bones and beats them together imitating the running of the buffalo and the rhythm of the hunt. All three of these men were expressing their personal experiences while hunting a buffalo to feed their families. These three different expressions represent the diversity with the fine arts. Theatre (drama) is created using the entire body to act out a story or interpret an experience through physical movement. Art represents a human expression using a media (paint, ink or stone) to create a representation of an idea. Examples of expression in art would be a painting by Goergia O'keefe, a glass sculpture by Dale Chihuly, or a drawing by a student in a classroom. Musical expression can be as simple as moving to the rhythm of a song or singing along to the radio or it could even be as intricate as playing an instrument creating a personal expression of the notes a composer created to express their own feelings in song. Artists are expressing feelings and emotions that create a work of art that relates to the common human bond that can be felt by anyone (see photo 1.1).

Esteban De Armas/Shutterstock.com

Photo 1.1

Human expression is a basic element of everyday life. Students within a classroom setting are constantly being asked to share and express ideas. Many times, these expressions are the means of interpreting the student's understanding of the lesson material. The process of expressing ideas begins with the ability to assemble thoughts in an orderly manner from the assortment of memories that have been stored within the brain. The accessibility of these thoughts is often clouded with the similarity of other thoughts. The sheer volume of these memories creates a sea of thoughts that are similar to one another; however, they are lacking any unique associations to make a particular memory stand out in order to access it quickly. Tagging memories with a unique association is referred to as **memory marking**. The process of marking memories for later retrieval is a frequently an overlooked task, but when implemented can improve a student's memory of subject matter. Fine arts experiences can be used to mark memories for students in educational settings.

Fine arts experiences employ several human senses (sight, sound, touch, etc.). The stimulation of these senses provides specific markers that are identified with the subject that is associated with the work of art. For instance, the color red is often associated with a stop sign or a fire hydrant. Memory markers for a stop sign might be recalled using the association of the octagonal shape of the sign as well as the color red. The brain employs a series of symbols to indicate certain traits that are common for objects. When a person observes a chair, their brain automatically evaluates the shape and qualities of the chair in order to determine what it might be. For example, a common feature for a chair would be a seating area sometimes with a back (see photo 1.2).

Photo 1.2 Three different chairs all have unique features, but can be placed in the single category of a chair

A student that is able to associate an unusual experience with a topic is more likely to retain that information long term. An example might be a teacher instructing students on ancient Greek theatre. In order to illuminate the content of the lesson, the teacher chose to dress in a toga and interpret the character of an ancient Greek actor. By creating the character of an ancient Greek actor, the teacher is able to not only capture the attention of the students in the classroom but also create an exceptional memory connection for the student that associates with ancient Greece. In the future when a student from that particular class is asked to recall information about ancient Greece, the memory of the teacher dressed in a toga will be associated with that lesson and improves the likelihood that the student will remember additional information that was given within that particular lesson.

The idea behind this type of teaching can easily be demonstrated by examining your own memories. Think about a vacation you took as a child. Perhaps it was to Washington, D.C., or the Rocky Mountains in Colorado. Wherever you traveled you collected mental souvenirs that are permanently linked to the location that you visited. For example, suppose a child travelling through Louisiana on the way to Florida purchased a carved wooden pelican at a stop in Shreveport, Louisiana. The pelican not only represented Louisiana but ultimately was linked as a reminder that the automobile had broken down providing time to shop for a souvenir. Fast forward 30 years and the child has grown into an adult but still has the carved pelican. It sits on a shelf in their office and any time they look at it they are reminded of the trip they took as a child and specifically the stop in Shreveport, Louisiana. Memories associated to this marker include the first trip to Louisiana, the automobile breaking down, a first encounter with a truck stop and the variety of people who were there, and the cool refreshing sensation of a cold Coca-Cola on a hot summer afternoon as it trickles down your throat. The Coca-Cola was a free gift from the cashier when the wooden pelican was purchased.

As you reflect on your own education as a child what sticks out in your memory? It is highly unlikely that a spelling lesson or even an ordinary grammar lesson will come to mind unless an unusual memory marker has been assigned to the memory. Creating memorable moments or mental souvenirs throughout a lesson cycle can improve student retention and increase learning by holding the student's attention.

Arts at Work

In 1975, a fourth-grade class was studying the settlement of Jamestown in a social studies unit. The teacher began by instructing the students to read the information in the textbook. After the students had read the material, the teacher showed a film that depicted the story of the Jamestown settlement. The class then discussed what they had read in the textbook and witnessed the same events through the magic of film the teacher instructed them to create a diorama depicting a single event involving the settlement of Jamestown. The students created the diorama then the teacher divided the class into four groups and instructed them to create a bulletin board about Jamestown. In addition to the bulletin board, the group was also instructed to develop a short presentation that depicted the settlement of Jamestown. All of these activities culminated in the celebration of the settlement of the Jamestown colony on May 13, 1607. The teacher invited parents to come and celebrate with the students.

May 13, 1975, was a special day for the students in that classroom. Memories were created that would forever be associated with the establishment of Jamestown. The students had used the arts to express what they were learning about the settlement of Jamestown. During the celebration that day, the parents were able to view the independent expression of each student. The classroom was decorated with artwork that each student had created. The bulletin boards and dioramas represented each student's personal interpretation of the history of the Jamestown settlement. As the parents arrived, the students were eagerly waiting to greet them and show them what they had accomplished. Cookies and punch were served and the students presented their short plays depicting the events of the settlement of Jamestown. The parents applauded and encouraged the students for their hard work and creative expression of the events that surrounded the settlement of the Jamestown colony.

Reading facts from a book creates a connection for some students, but employing the use of a variety of interactions with the material by using the arts creates a memorable experience that encourages longer retention of the knowledge. Researchers have found that integrating arts activities into classroom lessons encourages long-term retention of knowledge. In other words, a student can remember the details of a drawing or an improvisational acting scene depicting an event longer than reading words on a page.

Using the arts in the classroom allows the student to claim ownership in their own learning. The Jamestown assignment began with the student's interpretation of what they had discovered about Jamestown through the reading and the film that was viewed. Assigning the task to create a diorama immediately placed the responsibility of interpreting the information in the student's hands and allowed them to take complete control of their personal interpretation of what happened at Jamestown. As the students began to think about what to recreate in their diorama, they had to sift through the information that had been presented to them. After carefully reviewing the information, they settled on a single event to recreate through the artistic expression of a diorama.

Evolution of Evaluation

It is important to note at this point that in a classroom filled with 25 students creating a diorama there will be none that are exactly alike. The assignment involved a personal interpretation of the events at Jamestown encouraging the students to think creatively in order to express their personal ideas about Jamestown. Each student brings not only what they have studied about Jamestown but also everything they have experienced up to that point in their lives. The mind uses past experiences to evaluate and understand new material that is presented. Consider a young baby as they discover the new world around them. They reach out and touch and feel in order to evaluate and record what an object feels, tastes, and smells like. These memories are saved to be used at a later time to evaluate similar objects. For example, a baby might examine a red ball by touching, tasting, and examining it very closely. If a green ball is placed in front of them, they will eventually discover the similarities between the red and green ball. They both are round, feel, and taste the same; however, the color is different. As the child grows, they are able to make the assumption that each of the two objects is a ball even though they are different colors. If the two balls and an apple are placed on the table in front of a young child, they are able to determine the difference between the red ball and the apple by several factors. The apple has a distinct smell that is different from the red ball. The red ball has no distinct taste, but if the child investigates the taste of the apple, it can be determined that it is very different from the red ball. The texture of the ball is very different from the apple. As the child has grown, the memory of these investigations is applied in order to provide an instant analysis when a child encounters a ball or an apple in order to identify what it is. As the child encounters more objects memories are stored to aide in the future evaluation of new objects.

Thoughts from a Seasoned Artist

As a child growing up I always was fascinated by art. I loved trips to some of the most famous museums in the world and was always wondering how a painter would seem to make the objects and people look so realistic. I would come back to my elementary school and often ask my art teacher Mrs. Myers, how such was done. Her answer was always so encouraging; she would say "art such as that takes a lot of time and dedication." My understanding of this seemed simple. As a child I recall that I had lots of time, and felt quite dedicated to my art. After all, art was my favorite subject in school and my grades indicated that I was a successful student of art.

The first elementary school that I attended did not have a formal art room or teacher. It was up to the classroom teacher to provide art. Most of the teachers did not seem too interested in spending time on art. Oh yes, we did cut out things, color things, and draw a few stick people, but art, real art . . . seemed to evade most classrooms at this school. This changed when I moved and went to a new school in the fourth grade that seemed to open up the world of art for me along with all that it encompassed. The revelation of this new world of art started when I encountered what I considered to be a "master art teacher," Mrs. Myers. This older lady (who was probably not 40 years of age) spoke of the great art of the world. In the first week of school, I had already learned the story of Mona Lisa and of her importance in the field of art. Mrs. Myers had a way of telling the history of art that made every student want to understand and learn more. She told the story of art from the beginning with examples of the cave drawing in France done over 30,000 years ago right up to the 1960s and the wild posters of rock groups and figures of musicians like Jimi Hendrix.

Thoughts from a Seasoned Artist (*Continued*)

It was from this experience in a wonderful art room with an outstanding teacher that not only did I understand the history of art and all that could be learned from it but also the value that art really plays in the development of a child as a human being. The sensitivity that is learned through art and art history is a driving force that teaches people about human history and about life in general. Art tells a story, speaking volumes describing what a person feels, thinks, and cares most about. It was with this knowledge, that I began my real quest to not only learn as much as possible about this wonderful subject but also a belief that I would someday in some perhaps small way, inspire others to tell their story, through works of art.

Everyone Is an Artist

The fine arts are all rooted in human expression. Every person is capable of expressing emotions and ideas. The obstacle to creative expression is the thought that seems to be driven into children's head from an early age that anything that is created must be perfect and created exactly the same as someone else would create it. One possible culprit of this idea is the coloring sheet. Photocopies are made and passed out in the classroom and the children begin to color the picture of Santa Claus while listening to Christmas songs. After they have been carefully colored, the teacher collects them and displays them on the bulletin board in the room. Most of them are colored in the traditional red and white theme which eludes to most people's image of Santa Clause. Two students however did not choose to color Santa's suit red, one colored it bright yellow and another blue. When asked why they didn't color Santa correctly, the replies demonstrated that assumptions in the classroom can be unfair. One student did not know who Santa Claus was and had never been exposed to an image of Santa so the obvious choice for that child was bright yellow since that was her favorite color. The other child quickly responded that he had colored a picture of Elvis Pressley and his song "Blue Christmas" since that was playing in the room; therefore, Santa's suit was blue. The teacher more than likely expected to have 20 pictures of Santa that for the most part looked identical other than the coloring the student would do to complete them.

Consider the same project except change one variable. Instead of passing out a printed coloring sheet pass out a blank piece of paper. This truly allows the child to express their thoughts and creatively interpret their unique idea of Santa Claus. The printed coloring sheet may look more professional and perfect, but it lacks the child's individual interpretation.

Classrooms are filled with unique students bringing a variety of talents and gifts to share and develop. It is important for teachers to look for these unique abilities and encourage the students to grow and develop rather than to tell them they are stupid and will never succeed. A renowned neurological surgeon was told in elementary school that he was stupid and would never succeed. Even though his mother was illiterate she required her children to read books and write about them in reports for her to look over. The encouragement of an illiterate mother opened a door of possibilities for this young man. Reading developed his knowledge and ability resulting in a medical degree and a renowned practice as a neurosurgeon. This story should serve as a warning to educators that each student has potential and whether it is obvious or not it is the duty of the teacher to try and discover exactly what that potential might be. This surgeon was the first in his family to graduate from high school and go to college. Obviously, one teacher calling the student stupid did not keep him from succeeding, but what is not known is how many teachers did not call him stupid and instead encouraged him to succeed. A key to successful students is encouragement from the teacher. If a teacher expects greatness from the students in the classroom that is what will result. Expectations bring results. If the United States never expected to go to the moon, they would not have made it.

Encouraging students to develop their artistic ability allows them to fulfill not only their artistic potential but also their full mental capacity. Research has shown that when a person plays a musical instrument both sides of the brain are actively employed. Interpreting life through artistic expression allows us to examine who and what we are in an attempt to provide order and meaning to life. Every student has the potential to learn and grow in a classroom, but without the proper stimulation the seeds of creativity may lay dormant. Incorporating art, music and theatre into classroom lessons provides the much needed water to sprout the seeds of creativity.

CHAPTER 2
Expression within the Arts

Expression in its many forms has existed since the beginning of time. Each and every person wants to leave an impression even if it is not always a favorable one. Expression requires imagination. This can be difficult to cultivate in a society that has turned away from anything that requires time and thought, favoring the fast paced immediate feedback that technology offers. The ultimate goal of an educator should be prioritizing time to plan and implement strategies that will encourage creative expression among students within the classroom. Encouraging creative expression is crucial in order to encourage the appropriate intellectual and emotional develop of the student.

The fine arts are expressed in the many forms including visual arts, music, theatre and dance. The fine arts have not only given the human race a chance for individual recognition but also a collective voice based through culture, time periods, and events within society that should never be forgotten.

Beyond a beautiful dance, a wonderful painting, a score of music, or the lines from a script lies the hidden meaning that can be heard as an important voice often many times resulting in visionary ideas that help to shape the future. Through the Arts, self-discipline, motivation, and problem-solving skills are taught that will last a lifetime. When money and time are considered within a school board's decision making, it is often the Arts that are cut first. Rarely, if ever is the decision to cut an educational program made after carefully considering the impact on student expression. The provision for students to have a creative outlet for artistic expression is frequently overlooked within the decision-making process.

Truth in artistic expression is best explained as the freedom that is allowed for one to create something; not to be confused with being admired or respected. Consider a time in your own life where you were present at an event where the national anthem was being played and the crowd began to sing. Many times, there seems to be one voice louder than the others totally enraptured with the sound of their own voice totally unaware that others in the crowd are appalled that this person has no idea that they should lip sync the words rather than burden others with the horrendous sound of their voice. This lone person is demonstrating their expression of this meaningful song. Consider that it should not matter if they can't sing well, the reality is that the person is expressing pride for their country, rather than singing for an audition or anyone else's enjoyment. Next time you experience this phenomena consider enjoying the gusto and feeling of expression the person has rather than looking at them with a look of disgust. Artistic expression illuminates the individual and celebrates the tremendous power and potential to achieve greatness.

While visiting an art museum in Chicago in the 1980s, two women stood looking at a large painting by Jackson Pollack. One stated: "How on earth can this splashing of paint onto a large canvas be considered art!?" She seemed to be looking at the other woman for some type of answer or a tone of agreement. The other woman tried to carefully explain that it is not always just about the painting itself, but rather the idea or movement that is new that makes it a great piece. Then with a quizzical eye the woman replied, "You must be like all these other modern art fanatics, a kook!" It was shocking how quickly one person could judge another, but just like she judged the art quickly she judged the other woman quickly. This had nothing to do with Jackson Pollock's work or the woman, as a person that liked modern art. This had to do with the woman and her ability to step outside of her comfort zone and see something unique and different. When considering artistic expression, it must be free from the thoughts of what others may say or write about someone's personal expression within the arts.

Thoughts from a Seasoned Artist

When my daughter was age seven, she had been taking piano lessons for 2 years with a very accomplished piano teacher in the town where we lived. My daughter was a very good young pianist and learned very quickly the many different expectations of this famed older teacher. One afternoon about 2 days before a Christmas party recital at the teachers home, my daughter told me that she had decided to compose a piece rather than play what the teacher had suggested she play. I did not see any problem with that at all. I did not bother to let the teacher know of this change in plan, after all I was paying for these lessons and my daughter seemed to be going into the direction of a composer not just a pianist. I was thrilled. (Never having real piano lessons myself and wanting them, I was living my dream!) The night of the recital all of the children and parents took our places on folding chairs inside the lavish living room and sat in the shadow of the large grand piano. Children got up one by one and played the selected piece as the teacher called the child's name and the selection. As the teacher called my daughter up she announced her by name and also the pre-selected musical title. It was at that point that my daughter said she had composed her own piece that she would be playing. Keep in mind she was

Thoughts from a Seasoned Artist (*Continued*)

age seven. There was a gasp not only by the teacher but also by the other parents in the room. My daughter sat down and began to play what I considered to be fabulous. She was using high notes and low notes as well as the peddle. To me she sounded like a future Van Cliburn finalist! The piece wore on until a huge Crescendo at the end at which point I rose to my feet clapping. As I looked around the other parents sat looking disgusted. I then thought, "Well, it is obvious that there is jealously in the room because my child is a composer and your children can only play memorized pieces!" I went home happy my daughter had become a composer, even if I was the only one to recognize her talent and ability. More importantly, my daughter went home having self-expression exhibited on a stage in front of many a critic. It was the beginning of an inner voice for her to follow her dream and her heart as we all must if we can ever become authentic.

Artistic Expression Provides Unspoken Messages

We often wonder if we can get answers and information from a child when the level of vocabulary and understanding is still in the stage of infancy. Years ago a teacher had been approached to develop an art and P.E. program at a small private school where her children attended. She took on the challenge in large part due to her belief that all children needed these two outlets of expression. Young children learn about the world through observation and also interacting with each other. Two of the very best places for that in a school setting would be the art room and the gym. Not long after the semester began, the Teacher kept hearing the name of one young man repeated by the staff.

Jonathon was 5 years of age and should have been a part of both the art class and also the P.E. class. Unfortunately, Jonathan seemed to always be in some sort of trouble had not gotten the privilege of attending art or P.E. classes. Staying in trouble managed to keep him from participating in the "fun classes." The faculty all knew him and along with the headmistress, everyone seemed perplexed by the wild behavior. He hit and kicked both teachers and students alike. He ran away from adults and other children wanting to be his friend. He broke crayons in class, cut paper up, tore paper, and screamed loud shrieks for no reason. When confronted with this information by the headmistress of the school, the art teacher offered to have Jonathon come into the little makeshift art room and possibly through drawing and or conversation unlock the mystery of this little boy.

The art teacher was shocked when she saw Jonathon. He did not appear to be the wild tyrant that she had heard about. He was small for his age and had large blue eyes and sandy hair. His hair was silky and moved around a lot when he shook his head while talking. He liked to swing his legs while he spoke. They talked briefly about things he liked. He was quick to tell her about his dog and that he liked dogs better than people. He also informed her that he did not like tomatoes or corn on the cob. Although his school uniform looked like it had put in a hard day, Jonathon was as calm and serene as most anyone.

After careful observation, the teacher began to think perhaps there was nothing really wrong with Jonathon, other than he was accustomed to getting his way but was unable to handle things well if he did not. Most children at the school were somewhat spoiled, her own included, and some children just react in different ways when confronted by conflict. Jonathon would always go out of this way to speak to or give the art teacher a hug when he saw her in the hallway.

One afternoon the art teacher became aware of loud voices in the connecting hallway and went out to see what was going on. Jonathon was upset when the two classroom teachers were telling him it was almost time to go home, and he needed to wash his hands and put his jacket on. He broke free from the conversation and ran straight to the doorway to the art room. He announced to the art teacher that he did not want to go home. She quickly tried to remind him he would be seeing his dog Sassy and having something nice for dinner. Nothing seemed to calm him, so she instructed his teachers that he could stay with her in the art room until his mother came to pick him up.

She could see that Jonathon was still angry about something and suggested that he draw. Asking "Why don't you draw me a picture of Sassy?" With that, he took a sheet of white paper and a pencil and began to draw a large oval shape with four long stick like legs and large feet. Then he added a round head with triangle ears. They did not look like ears, but one could understand the meaning behind their shape. Sassy had some brown spots along her back followed by a tail that was far too big for a dog that size. Sassy had a smile on her face. A smile was something that had been missing from Jonathon in all the times the art teacher had seen him, yet Sassy could smile. She found this very odd. It was obvious that Sassy was happy even if Jonathon was not.

Then she suggested that he draw his family. As she glanced over at him, she noticed an intensity in that way that he was working on the family portrait. When he finished, he called her over to look at it. With one look at the drawing, a sudden awareness revealed that the answers to all of the questions she had about this puzzling little boy were soon to be answered. On the left was a large figure much taller than the other two. One arm was extended way beyond the length of the other arm. The face had been scribbled out. In the middle, a much smaller shaped person. Long faced with a very sad frown that extended beyond what would be a normal mouth line. Next was a figure, taller than the last but again with the large frown and sad eyes. Over the head were marks and lots of them. My, how this picture spoke volumes.

The teacher assumed nothing because she wanted Jonathon to explain these people if possible. She asked Jonathon who the person was with the scratched out face. "That is Dad," he said. Pointing to the small shrunken middle figure, with the clown-sized frown, she asked about the next figure. "That is me," he said as if she should recognize him instantly. This person on the end, is this Mom? Yes, that is her. "Can you not see she is crying?" A closer examination revealed that some tears were drawn under the eyes. She then redirected his attention back to "Dad. Why is one of his arms so much longer than his other, Jonathon?" He replied, "Oh, That is not just his arm; he is holding the wooden spoon. Didn't you see where he hit Mom on the head?" As she looked back at the figure on the right with the sad face with tears, she noticed the strike marks above the head. Jonathon then explained that Dad made a regular habit of hitting both he and Mom with a wooden spoon.

Through this crude, yet telling drawing the mystery of the wild and erratic behavior of Jonathon had been fully explained. This young boy lived in a volatile home, filled with anything money could buy, but without any safety or stability. Both he and his mother were living the life of the sad figures that stared back at the art teacher from the cheap drawing paper. His blue eyes had seen things no one could want to see or experience. At five his drawing was realistic and filled with emotion.

The teacher made a copy of the drawing and kept the original but gave the copy to the headmistress of the school who gave it to Child Protective Services. Soon after that, Jonathon went into foster care until his parents divorced and then he and his mother moved away. Years later, the teacher learned that he had graduated from college with a degree in social work. He had escaped the ugly situation and had become a successful member of society. Even though Jonathan encountered the art teacher for a brief time in his life, it had a lasting impact on him.

Courtesy Jodie Schenck

Jonathan's drawing

How many Jonathans are out there in classrooms silently living with a nightmare at home? How will their story end? On a positive note, or will the anger in them rage and ruin what could become a wonderful future? Perhaps only their art work can unlock the secrets and predict that. It is important to consider that art is an expression that is founded in truth.

Encouraging Artistic Expression within the Classroom

One of the main reasons artistic expression needs to be encouraged within the classroom is that for many children it is artistic expression that helps them remember key points. When a child sits and works only from a book or copied worksheet, there is little stimulation to help remember or enjoy what is being taught. The blending of the arts goes far beyond art, music, and theate. There are ideas in teaching that blend what is needed to learn in different classes with movement, acting, and writing scripts, as well as showing the balance of a painting in comparison to balance on a scale in science.

When students are participating in learning rather than just listening, they do enjoy it and remember it. What has driven the American classroom to become so boring for the students sitting at the desks? The lack of excitement has encouraged discipline to become an issue because students are tired of hearing the same things over and over as well as not enjoying or relating to what is being learned. Rarely if ever is a lesson presented and related to real-life experiences. Educators are spending far too much time telling students information rather than giving them the tools to seek knowledge, develop individual questions, and actually check for student understanding. Simply asking students questions from time to time can encourage the students to search for individual meaning within the subject matter.

Young children all love to draw or paint a picture to go along with a book that they have read. Upper elementary children seem to do well-writing small scripts to solve problems within the school day. An example of a script would be students writing about how to include the new student into the classroom. By having to stop and think and write ways to make a new student feel welcome, the actions shown to the new student are embedded into their young minds making it much easier to remember when a new student comes into and already established class.

Each and every child has some gift that is often dormant until a spark is offered by a creative, motivated teacher that knows that there is more than one way to teach. A teacher who varies instructional style also encourages a safe haven in which to try new things without ridicule. By having all students engaged in trying new things and supporting their peers in the process, it establishes a very democratic classroom. This also encourages walls between students to be removed and preconceived ideas about other students to melt away. In place of the walls, new bridges are built allowing learning to take place.

Once years ago when break dancing was just making its appearance among young people trying new ways to express themselves; a future star dancer was on a team of students. A book was being read in class that talked about some young kids growing up on the south side of Chicago who started break dancing for money on the street. After the class finished the book, the teacher allowed students to come up with their own ideas and to form their own groups to determine how to best explain the book without writing a dreaded "book report."

One group of boys decided to act out a couple of the scenes from the book and write their own dialogue. In this group was a young teenage boy named Antonio who was not only good at break dancing but very handsome as well. As he spun around on the floor of the classroom going through his entire dance moves a star was born! The students loved the script that the boys wrote and also the dance that followed it. Weeks after that performance, the teacher began to hear about how Antonio was not doing his work in his other classes but was spending time practicing new dance moves. Before long his grades were dropping and his parents were getting reports from school.

Following up on this issue Antonio's father came to school one afternoon after he had worked all day to get needed answers of what had happened to Antonio's grades. He came to school in his work clothes, work boots and a hat that kept his head shaded from the hot sun and heat. Upon entering the classroom, he encountered four team teachers sitting in a semicircle ready to speak about grades, also sitting quietly in a chair was Antonio. The contrast of Antonio and his father was obvious. The father had a tired worn look and thick hands that showed the hard calluses of long hours of hard work over many years. His English was broken but understandable even with the heavy Spanish accent. Antonio sat straight up with a body full of energy which was reminiscent of the previous weeks dance routine his group had done that brought the entire class to their feet. Antonio had as much energy as a lightning bolt. His clothes were cleaned and pressed. Even after a full day at school his shirt and jeans held their shape with what must have been tremendous starch. It was obvious that his mother must have worked late into the night ironing his clothes to make sure that his school appearance was perfection.

When Antonio's father began to speak, he apologized to the teachers for his broken English. They all smiled and encouraged him to continue. Each teacher took a turn at letting him know the many assignments that Antonio was missing and his average that had dropped significantly. When all of the teachers had finished speaking, the father hung his head a moment and then began to speak directly to Antonio.

"Look at these hands that have worked all day in the hot sun so you could get your education in this country!" "Look at how hard your mother has worked to dress you in clean, pressed clothes to come to this school and get the education we did not get in our country!" "How is it, that you come here and not do your work for these ladies?" Is it time Antonio, for you to leave this place and pick up a shovel and work as I have?" Suddenly from his chair Antonio spoke. "No Papa, I will start to do my work. I know how much you and Mama have sacrificed for me to get a good education." I will start doing less dancing and complete my school work." He then jumped up and hugged his father. Both were in tears.

Is it possible that bringing creativity into an assignment fostered Antonio's dance obsession. This example demonstrates that when students have the opportunity to become creative after a long time spent without a creative outlet it can frequently cause students to become obsessed with expression to their own detriment. Therefore, from the earliest age, classroom educators should offer a chance to explore the talent and gifts of students in order to allow them to develop creative expression progressively rather than awakening these skills later in life and developing an obsession.

Art Is Expression for Young and Old Alike

While art can speak for the very young, it can also speak for the fractured and tormented teen. A middle school art teacher observed after many years teaching that she had spent countless hours viewing the "free drawings and paintings" that his students loved to do. As they often would ask: "When can we paint and draw what we like, and not do a planned assignment?" One afternoon while collecting the "free" paintings from the drying rack, a painting caught the teacher's attention. It was a large piece of paper with a muddied red and black tempera wash with the words" I want to die" scratched into the paint. The teacher frantically picked up the painting still wet with paint and went searching for a name . . . Not on the front, not on the back, not hidden in code . . . Not even a class period listed. The teacher began to think back through the day trying desperately to remember who was painting with red and black, who had asked for red or black. As his mind raced trying to decipher who this mystery student was as sense of urgency overcame him. Was this perhaps a cry for help or for someone to notice the pain the student was feeling? A sense of helplessness overcame him as he realized his inability to rescue this young person. The night was spent hoping that no harm came to this young person, and that time would allow the teacher to find the student the following day.

Each class period, he purposefully held several paintings captive until a student came forward to declare ownership or ask about their missing painting. By the end of period four, all captive paintings had been claimed except one. Yes, the sad and lonely one of red and black remained. As the fifth period students arrived for class and were coming in it was obvious that one of them was the artist who created this lone work. The teacher knew it had to be in this class that the mystery would be solved. This was the last class that had painted the day before.

After a brief talk about the next lesson, with a sense of great relief that for a time the students would not be working on free art, a student looked up with woeful eyes and said, "I can't find my painting." The teacher then asked the question, "What does it look like?", in hopes that it would lead to a more intimate conversation about the painting. Does it have your name on it? The student replied, "It is red and black and does not have my name." As the teacher handed her the painting, he asked if they could visit outside about it and the upcoming art show. She seemed pleased that her work had sparked interest. The teacher calmly explained to her that he was moved by her painting and concerned about the message of the painting. The teacher wanted to offer help and support for what appeared to be a cry for help as well as understanding and comfort. She explained that she had been going through some rough things at home, and most of it had worked out that it was only a frustrated, scribbled notation that depicted the feelings about her day. At first, the teacher felt relieved and wondered if he had simply overreacted. Later, as he thought about it on the drive home, he decided that it was better to take action and investigate than wonder what could have been said or done to prevent disaster.

Later on that semester, the teacher had reminded the students about the upcoming art show that would highlight their work for the public to see. Many grand and wonderful things came in, but when it was mentioned that students could also sell their art if they chose. The amount of art entries soon increased tenfold!

The teacher asked Alice if she would be willing to sell him the red and black painting. She agreed and the deal was struck. Alice was thrilled that a teacher, especially her art teacher, would want to purchase her work. After Alice sold her artwork to the teacher, he began to notice the subject of her drawing and painting was a fetus! After overcoming the shock of the subject, the teacher realized that it was actually a quite good and accurate rendition of life at the earliest stage! Realizing that the school would not approve of the painting for display in the art show, he quickly asked "Alice" if this painting of the fetus was also for sale. Alice quickly replied, "Yes," but the price had now doubled! To keep an uprising from coming down from the school principal, the teacher paid her ransom. Meanwhile, other paintings kept coming in, teachers were buying teapots, flowers, dogs and cats, and trees of all colors and sizes, and it was still a week away from the public show. Each passing day brought more art to see and sell and it was a grand time for students, teachers, and the public. "Alice" continued working at home on some animals, a mask, a waterfall, and a stone bridge. The teacher observed the potential for her to possibly selling all of her work. Other students were even offering to buy some of her things, she was perceived as an artist on the rise. While collecting the final pieces to put up on display, Alice brought in what would be her last painting. Having watched Alice create some of the most interesting works of art, the teacher stared at what would become the third piece in his new collection.

Another painting from the abyss of the womb. This time though not one fetus but two. These two perfectly drawn and painted voyagers were floating free in a circle of liquid only tethered by a cord that bound them to life. The teacher quickly picked up the painting and announced that it was his and shelled out more money for painting that created a trilogy of work by Alice. Proud of the money and new found fame she had acquired, Alice walked out into the displays of art glancing at others' work seeming to feel superior. Her life as the teacher observed over the past few months was reminiscent of a roller coaster the teacher had once ridden and was deathly afraid of. As it raced and rolled along the silver rails thrashing and throwing all upon it, never knowing what would come next. Just as the rollercoaster had thrown the teacher about, Alice had been able to paralyze him with the same type of fear. Alice had created artwork that gripped him, and made him think and fear, as well as making him spend money for something he did not understand. The one thing he did understand was that there once was a girl who hated her life for an instant that felt like an eternity, who felt sadness, who was linked to her past as a fetus, and then to a twin who could possibly take on some of the pain or the fame of her new identity as an artist. The teacher had been a part of her story. Years later looking on the walls of his office, the teacher observes these three paintings' by this young, fragile girl. He thinks of young Alice, who now is a woman and wonders if she was able to maintain the balance that she found in her young life, or did the past overtake her and tumble you over the rails on the rollercoaster of her life?

Enemies of Creativity in the Classroom

The main enemy of creativity in a classroom or anywhere else for that matter is fear. This is not the type of fear you might feel if walking alone in a dark alley but rather a fear that comes from the possibility of ridicule brought on by self-consciousness. Every person should have the freedom to feel that their idea or concept is good and meaningful. When a student is faced with the knowledge that their work will be subjected to ridicule as a result of grading or even a public viewing of the work it opens causes many students to shut down and an inability to think much less produce an expression in the form of an artwork.

This fear is rooted in an expectation that have evolved over the past 30 years as society has developed an emphasis that every child is a winner. Although this idea was meant to encourage a child by bolstering self-esteem, it has created a side effect that destroys the possibility for creativity. The fear of not winning creates a nervous tension that prevents creative thought. So many young people feel that they must "win" at everything rather than exploring the "truth" of personal creative expression. Frequently young children go home after a soccer match having never touched the ball and are given a trophy. This type of behavior really began in the 1980s when a persons' self-esteem became more important than the out-put of personal effort. A classroom full of students who grow up and sitting in an arena of doubt is strictly limited resulting in a majority that is not able to fully function.

How must we proceed to allow students to think freely, ask new questions, and explore new ideas? First it is up to the teacher to let students know that the goal is not always to produce outstanding artistic work but rather explore new possibilities and learn from them.

Many teachers will use a rubric for the visual arts. Nothing can shut down the idea of creativity faster than to give a rubric. When given a rubric, students follow it checking off each and every demand. Much like using a cookbook, if I do this and then this . . . my outcome will meet with success. What happens is not a surprise. The teacher will then get a room full of work that all looks the same with little differences. The teacher will then look at the outcome and comment to other teachers: "These kids today have no creativity or individual expression!" How could there be differences when a "prescription" of sorts was given to produce a known outcome. Many students who thought of coming up with a different approach became self-conscious when they looked around the room and thought their idea was too different and began to follow the group of work around them. Much like sheep trained to follow the shepherd no one wants to get out of line.

Many years ago when teaching painting, the goal was to teach the color wheel and how to use it correctly. Most schools spend so little time in the visual arts that children often know very little about color and how to make it. Starting with the primary colors and explaining that these cannot be made from mixing; going into the secondary colors and how we add two primaries to make a secondary. (Yellow + red= orange, blue + yellow= green, blue + red= violet.) The next item on the agenda would be to begin to teach the tertiary colors such as blue +green = blue-green.

Oh how the students loved mixing paint. Many could mix perfect and beautiful secondary and tertiary colors with little effort. If someone mixed something either by accident or on purpose resulting in a new color. Other students might watch in amazement waiting to see if this would be acceptable. It was important that the teacher state that even though this was not a chosen color to make, there was value in all colors and then encourage them to use some of the "new" colors in their work. In order to encourage the creative development of new colors the students were then encouraged to participate in a naming contest for the new colors. This process established the possibility to allow students to do something new with an old concept of paint mixing.

The freedom that this allowed students helped to boost their confidence as they became more successful in the expression of their artwork. It is up to the teacher to direct where creativity can go. Open ended ideas and concepts given to students give them permission to think without walls to break down and above all fear to overcome.

The fear of creativity can be realized in each person when they are asked to perform in front of a crowd. Whether it is singing a song or delivering a speech the fear of failure can be overwhelming. Although the possibility for every human to create music exists, many people are crippled by the idea that they are not musical. Music is not just based in pitch, but rhythm is a key component to musical expression. When a person listens to a song, they have the ability to express the feeling of the music through movement, tapping, or evening clapping their hands. Musical ability is not based on perfect pitch but rather a connection to the music.

Drama is also a natural ability that each person has perfected as they have grown each day. A key example of this would be the simple question that two friends might share; How do I look? The answer to this question may be based in reality or a complete fabrication in order to spare the other person's feelings. If the answer is based on a slight falsehood then the person must present facial and physical expressions that emphasize the truth of the false statement. Daily interactions among people are filled with theatrical activity.

Humans are taught as they grow that physical expression can manipulate others. This manipulation can be as simple as the cry of a baby who is hungry or as intricate as a child who is frowning because they do not like something. Children naturally are drawn to imitation. Creative play encourages artistic expression. An example is children playing school. One child is the teacher and the others are the students. The role of the teacher is played with intricate detail recalling the knowledge the child has gained that relates to teachers. Children naturally recreate scenes and situations as a form of play.

Fear in the Classroom

The classrooms of today in all subject areas not just the visual arts are being critically and unfairly influenced and directed by many teachers in education who teach through fear. Fear is the opposite of trust. When someone is afraid of a person or an assignment then the authenticity of the outcome comes under question. The work that is presented represents what the student thinks the teacher wants to hear, rather than what the student knows or believes. Belief in personal ideas and ability goes away when biting criticism is used when talking about the importance of what is to be done or explaining an assignment. When this occurs students slowly begin speak and express themselves less. Students begin to copy more and depend on others more for support and encouragement. The student's own independent voice of creativity is rendered mute by the fear that what is original and their own is not good enough.

In experiments conducted by psychologist Theresa Amabile, the conditions of what might increase or decrease creativity were studied. Some of the experiments asked the participants, who were frequently children, to produce some creative product. The creative product might be a poem, a drawing, short story, play, or rhythm. After the participant created the product, it was then evaluated for creativity by a group of experts. Even though creativity is hard to define, it is easily recognizable. The judges were quite consistent in their evaluations of the work even though they judged them independently. They consistently liked the original, shocking, meaningful, and coherent. Original products that originate with random thoughts were not scored as creative since the thoughts had not been developed intentionally into the product.

In some of Amabile's experiments, she would divide the group, telling some their work would be judged and the most creative would be awarded prizes; and the other part of the group would be told nothing. The results of these experiments were very consistent. In experiment after experiment, the products judged the most creative came from the group that did not know they were being evaluated. The results of a task that requires creativity, new ideas or the learning of new concepts, usually are far better when the artist is not aware that final product will be evaluated. Evaluation promotes effort that is based on trying to impress the evaluator. Effort to impress suppresses creativity. Rarely can someone become more creative just by working harder. To become creative, you must pull away from self and allow unconscious processes to work. The creative process should include fun while playing around or experimenting with ideas rather than looking for praise. Removing restrictions allows creativity to flourish.

Evaluation and fear go hand in hand as an enemy to creativity. It is not difficult to see why children have become less creative as schools across the United States have continued to encourage more and more testing. Testing that is not interested in measuring the true ability of the student, but rather in order to give the appearance of success for the school as a whole. A person who takes education seriously finds that ongoing testing and evaluations are creating a continued threat to students.

Students' minds are always alert to a score or some measurement of how they look. How do I please this teacher, how do I score better on this test? It is next to impossible to be or become creative in this type of environment. Student success should be the focus in the classroom rather than obtaining a high testing score. Student expression should be encouraged in order to fully develop their minds and open the door to limitless possibilities.

CHAPTER 3
Art in the Classroom

The Availability of Art

Having the ability to have art has changed over the decades as education has evolved. In the 1960s, children in the public schools of major cities went to the art classroom daily. One such room was taught by Mrs. Meyers a veteran teacher in every way measurable. This room was filled with huge windows adorned with window shades that could be used to keep out glare or direct sunlight during long afternoons. Mrs. Meyers believed in organization in all aspects of the classroom. Children sat by the letter of their last name. Paper was placed in the cabinet according to color with lightest colors on top descending to darker colors on the bottom. Glue bottles were arranged by size as to what age child would be using it. Crayons were kept in a neat box that did not allow for rolling off the table. Pencils also were boxed by size in circumference. Great art was born of this room primarily due to the fact that Mrs. Meyers having been highly organized was also a real planner when it came to the art projects and what we would be doing on any given week or day. On a chalk board weekly was printed the outline of what was to come. This type of planning gave excitement to the classroom. Mrs. Meyers was an older lady with a bun on the back of her head and reading glasses on the tip of her nose or hanging from a chain around her neck. She wore an apron with many pockets and could remedy any problem facing a young artist by reaching in one of the many pockets and producing a quick fix. Mrs. Meyers had energy far beyond her years. Her car could be seen late in the evening on the parking lot and her small frame visible through the windows as she scurried around the room getting ready for the next day and group of classes she would face. Children loved to go into the art room and she loved to have us. She enjoyed her job and children enjoyed learning from this imaginative individual.

Remember this was the 1960s when the Kennedy administration in the White House had a definite belief in the Arts and pushed it in schools across America from the earliest of elementary schooling into all colleges that were accepting federal money. The Arts were important! Schools today tend to not want to spend money on the Arts but rather provide money for another test or venue that is thought to have more merit. Art classes, music classes, and theatre classes have mostly been cut in public schools replaced by afternoon tutoring times, story hour, and different sport camps. Many highly qualified teachers have been removed from their positions within the Arts and told they would teach one of their other certified areas of knowledge or encourage making a transition to a new district that still was running a full art curriculum.

Aliens in the Arts

With all of the shuffling within the Arts one, other idea has come into play. The student who takes classes involving Arts; sometimes is not really an interested party but one that has been pushed over into this space of allotted class time because a talent for sports was not evident or the math tutoring room was full. What happens next is that a child without any prior knowledge of the Arts is forced to become a part of a world they are unsure of and concerned about a grade that might possibly reflect the lack of ability. (Having been possibly the only person to ever be told that they could not be a part of their church Christmas Cantata unless I would agree to just be a town's person and lip sync I understand this feeling!)

This becomes the scenario in which real teachers can make a huge impact and hopefully it will be a positive one. In all of the areas of the Arts, there can be hidden talent and desire to learn and become better. It is the most important job for a teacher to find and extract that mystery and help to develop it.

Natural Designers

The very youngest of children coming into school are at the kindergarten age. Many have had the opportunity at home for experimentation with art materials but many have not. The kindergarten teacher wanting to start the process of integrating the Visual Arts must understand what can be expected at this early age. The Kindergarten student is a natural design expert. They feel as though they know what they are doing and why they are doing it in a certain way. This often times is nothing more than scribbles however the scribbles are given names of objects they are drawing or painting. The teacher and or adult observer must understand that positive feedback and encouragement is the only thing that will help them to stick with their drawings until they can get better. Anything that is said to challenge their ability will cause them to shut down and not continue. With color they understand the difference between bright and dull as well as dark and light. They will choose to use a color based on what colors they like rather than what they know to be more realistic. The colors of the sky can be red or green and grass can be orange or purple. Most may know the primary colors of red, yellow, and blue but will be shocked to see two of the primaries mixed together to make a new color called secondary.

To take blue and mix yellow with it to make the color green will result in an outcry of excitement and wonder. They then will ask "What two colors can be mixed to make red?" (Often a favorite color of the very young.) They are disappointed when told that a primary like red cannot be mixed and can only be found in its purest form from minerals in the earth. The kindergarten student knows thin and thick lines, and most geometric shapes. The child will often draw the outside of a building and the inside as well in the same picture plane. Spacing of objects does not seem important at this stage in artistic development.

Color, Texture, and Creative Expression

First- and second-grade students begin to look at color more realistically especially as a student is moving closer to second grade. They understand texture of objects in nature. They can look at a picture of a feather and see that is would feel different than sand on the beach. It is important for the visual art teacher to have many objects to offer young students to look at and examine to determine different qualities. For that child who has had limited exposure to a variety of places or objects providing access these object in the created center of sensory items is most helpful. This age of child understands balance in a picture as well as what would make a certain object the most important part of a drawing or painting. Understands light and dark but does not fully appreciate value in shading. This age child can draw a feeling that goes with the sound of a song or musical instrument as well as an emotional feeling that is personal.

Understanding Shadows and Movement

The third- and fourth-grade student understands shading and that light from one side causes shadows on the other. They understand that lines are what can show movement within art. More use of diagonal lines and jagged lines introduced. This young artist is able to understand foreground, middle ground, and background and the importance of each. Can place objects in the overlapping state to show which is closest to the eye of the viewer. Has no trouble of painting a monochromatic painting using the different values of the same color to get the desired effect. (pale blue skin, darker blue hair, darkest blue eyelashes, etc.) Likes to work with the opaque paints but also enjoys the transparent look of watercolor. Often times caves into frustration with the watercolor not staying put on the paper but running with the water. It is up to the teacher to show where these types of "mistakes" are not really mistakes at all but rather can be used to show interest using added color and texture to add definition to the work of art. Understands the difference in two- and three-dimensional space and feels comfortable to draw in two-dimensional format and build the object into a three-dimensional form.

Artistic Detail

Fifth- and sixth-grade students can use converging lines to show perspective and have mastered the use of detail to show interest. Understands what is meant by portrait, and figure drawing. Can use cones, triangles, and other geometric shapes to compose sketches for final drawing. Students at this age can take a simple shape and turn it into an abstract object. Use of cartoons and made up figures become important. Designing of new items that are used today becomes a welcomed challenge. Interest in space as a subject or the ocean is also subjects of interest. Can use all of the artistic elements to create interesting works. The fifth- and sixth-grade student can use positive and negative spaces along with size and scale. The use of overlapping can be used and understood to show depth perception in realistic and abstract space. Can mix colors to come up with desired color needs and has a wide use of shades and tints to achieve their artistic goals. The use of multi-medium works of art is of great interest. Artist at this age are eager to help their fellow students to get maximum results and offer ideas that can benefit solving a dilemma. The fifth- and sixth-grade student has interest in the timeline of the art world and the study of different cultures and their importance in the field of art.

The Vocabulary of Visual Art Terms

It is very important that fifth- and sixth-grade students begin to learn the correct terms in the language of art.

Aesthetics—A branch of philosophy that focuses on the nature of beauty, the nature, and value of art and the inquiry process and human responses associated with those topics.

Art analysis—identifying and examining separate parts as they function independently and together in creative works and studies of the visual arts.

Art content—What the artwork is about, the idea of intended meaning.

Art criticism—Describing and evaluating the media, processes, ideas, history, subject matter, symbols, themes, and meanings of works of visual art and making comparative judgments.

Art elements—The visual arts components of line, value, shape, space, color, pattern, and texture.

Art history—A record of the visual arts, incorporating information, interpretations, and judgments about art objects, artists, and conceptual influences on developments in the visual arts.

Art materials—Resources used in the creation and study of visual art, such as paint, clay, cardboard, canvas, film, videotape, models, watercolors, wood, and plastic.

Art media—Broad categories for grouping works of visual art according to the art materials used.

Assess—To analyze and determine the nature and quality of achievement through means appropriate to the subject.

Context—A set of interrelated conditions such as time, place, purpose, influence, function, style, and social, economic, and political conditions in the visual arts that influence and give meaning to the development of thoughts, ideas, or concepts and that define specific cultures.

Create—To produce works of visual art using materials techniques, processes, elements, and analysis. The flexible and fluent generation of unique, complex, or elaborate ideas.

Description—Facts about the subject and who, when, where, and how the artwork was created. This includes the time and place, climate, resources, ability to communicate ideas of the times, themes, symbols used, and technology. It also includes knowledge of the media, techniques, and processes and what makes them effective or not in expressing the intent of the artwork.

Design principles—The underlying organizational characteristics in the visual arts: balance, dominance, rhythm, contrast, harmony, variety, and unity.

Evaluation—Reflecting on and forming a judgment and then validating reasons for choices regarding a work of art.

Expression—A process of conveying ideas, feelings, and meanings through selective use of the communicative possibilities of the visual arts.

Expressive qualities—Elements evoking affects such as joy, sadness, or anger. There are sensory, formal, and individual qualities.

Ideas—A formulated thought, opinion, or concept that can be represented in visual or verbal form.

Interpretation—Ways to understand the art work either the students own or others. This includes responding to the artwork's meaning, function, purpose, and value.

Perception—Visual and sensory awareness, discrimination and integration of impressions, conditions, and relationships with regard to objects feelings and images.

Process—A complex operation involving a number of methods or techniques, such as the addition and subtraction process in sculpture, the etching and intaglio processes in printmaking or the casting and construction process in making of jewelry.

Structures—Means of organizing the components of a work into a cohesive and meaningful whole, such as sensory qualities, design principles, expressive qualities, and functions of art.

Synesthesia—A mental image that corresponds to something that is entirely different, that is when one hears a certain sound a particular color comes to mind.

Techniques—Specific methods of approaches used in a larger process. For example, graduation in value or color in painting or conveying linear perspective through overlapping shading or varying size or color.

Technologies—Complex machines used in the study and creation of art, such as lathes, presses, computers, lasers, or video equipment.

Tools—Instruments and equipment used to create and learn about art, such as brushes, scissors, brayers, easels, knives, cameras, and kilns.

Visual arts—A very broad category that includes the traditional fine arts, such as drawing painting, printmaking, and sculpture; communication and design arts such as the film, television , graphics, and product design; and architecture and environmental arts, such as urban, interior, and landscape design. Ceramics, fibers, folk art, jewelry, work in wood, paper, and other materials.

Vocabulary of Visual Art Elements

Line: a horizontal, vertical, angled, or curved mark, across a surface. (Long, short, dotted.)

Shape: the two dimensions of height and width arranged geometrically (circles, triangles,) organically (natural shapes), symbolically (letters).

Color: hue means color names. Primary, secondary, and complementary; warm (red/yellow) and cool (blue/green).

Value: lightness (tints) or darkness (shades) of colors.

Saturation: vibrancy/purity vs dullness of color.

Space: the two-dimensional area that objects take up (positive space) and that surround shapes and forms (negative space); in-depth illusions are created by techniques such as perspective and overlapping.

Texture: way something feels or looks as it would feel (slick, rough)

Form: three dimensions (height, width, and depth) shown by contours (sphere, pyramid, and cube)

Art Concepts and Design Principles

Composition: arrangement of the masses and spaces. Foreground, middle, and background: the areas in a piece of art that appear closest to the viewer, next closest, and farthest away.

Structures and forms: two dimensions—art with length and width, such as paintings or photography; three dimensions art also has height/depth, such as sculpture.

Balance: weight of elements distributed symmetrically or asymmetrically.

Emphasis: areas that are stressed and attract the eye.

Variety: no two elements used are the same.

Repetition: elements used more than once (shapes, lines) create pattern and texture.

Contrast: opposition or differences of elements (created by light colors next to dark).

Rhythm/motion: sense that there are paths through the work.

Unity: the sense there is a whole working together.

Light: illusion created with lighter colors.

Vocabulary of Balance

Symmetrical balance—The balance achieved when there is equal distribution of forces on both sides of a picture.

Asymmetrical balance—The balance achieved when there is unequal distribution of forces on either side of the drawing creates an overpowering feeling, a heavy weight.

Radial balance—The balance achieved when all of the art elements radiate from a central point. In nature, radial balance is exemplified in the petals of a daisy or the cross section of a grapefruit.

Weight—The perceived heaviness of an object or art element. Weight often depends on location, size, shape, color, and relationships to other art elements.

Vocabulary of Color

Achromatic—A color scheme using white, gray, and black.

Analogous colors—Colors that are side by side on the color wheel and that are similar in hue, such as red, red-orange, and orange.

Chroma—The brilliance or intensity of color

Color advance and recede—The effect achieved when color is sensed as being in front of or in back of another color. Warm colors advance, cool colors recede.

Color balance—The color arrangement in a design that indicates harmony or disharmony.

Color blend—The effect achieved when two similar colors are placed side by side.

Color contrast—The effect achieved when two distinctly different colors are placed side by side.

Color effect—The effect achieved when a color impression is conveyed to the viewer through the use of color.

Color purity—The degree of maximum strength of any given color.

Color relativity—The quality of color that is dependent on the color's relationship to other colors.

Cool colors—green, blue, violet, and derivatives.

Complementary colors—Colors that when used side by side such as red next to green offer the visual illusion of maximum contrast. On a color wheel, complementary colors are opposite one another. Red is opposite green, blue is opposite of orange, and yellow is opposite of violet. When opposites are mixed, complementary colors are "grayed" or neutralized. Artist often gray colors this way, rather than adding black or white to the color.

Hue—The classification or name of a color. Artist often uses the word hue to indicate color. Technically, the hue of an object is the wavelength of light reflected from it. When the reflected wavelength of light changes, the color changes.

Intensity—The strength of weakness (brightness or dullness) of a color. Sometimes, it is called the saturation chroma. A hue that is not mixed with any other color is at its maximum intensity. Bright red, for example, has greater intensity than brown or dark blue.

Monochromatic—Describes all of the shades, tints, values, and intensities of one color.

Opaque—With regard to color describes a thin, transparent, watered down use of paint or ink

Pigment—The coloring matter that is mixed with oil, water, wax, and other substances to make paints, crayons, chalks, etc.

Primary colors—Red, yellow, and blue—the colors that cannot be made by mixing other hues and from which all secondary colors are created.

Related colors—Personal selection of colors that go well together.

Secondary colors—The colors that contain amount equal amounts of two primary colors; yellow and blue make green, blue and red make violet, and yellow and red make orange.

Shade—A color that is darkened by adding black. Example, maroon is a shade of red.

Spectrum—The continuum of color formed when a beam of white light is dispersed, as by passage through a prism, into red, orange, yellow and blue, indigo, and violet.

Tertiary colors—Colors that are a result of mixing unequal amounts of two primary colors (for example, a green that is produced by mixing more yellow than blue) or mixing primary and secondary colors (for example, the red-violet produced by mixing red and violet).

Tint—a color that is lightened and whose intensity is reduced by adding white. For example, pink is a tint of red.

Tone—A color to which both black and white have been added.

Value—Describes the amount of light or dark contained in the color on a scale ranging from black to white. Adding white to a color lightens the value. Adding black to a color darkens the value.

Warm colors—Red, orange, yellow, and derivatives.

Vocabulary of Light

Illumination—The amount of light reflected by an object illumination depends on the brightness of the light source and on the distance between the light and the receiving object.

Opaque—Describes objects and materials, such as people and buildings that stops light waves. Opaque materials cast shadows.

Reflection—The return of light waves from a surface. On smooth or shiny surfaces, light is changed from its normal straight line and bounced off (reflected) at an angle. On uneven surfaces, light is reflected in many directions by small surfaces reflecting at various angles.

Refraction—Light goes through different materials at different speeds. The bending of light waves from their normal straight path as they pass from one medium into another.

Shadow—Determined by the size of the light source, the number of light sources, the size of the opaque object, and the size or length of the angle at which the light hits the opaque object.

Transparent—Describes materials, such as glass, air, and water, that permit light to pass through them unchanged. Transparent materials do not cast shadows.

Vocabulary of Space

Color variation—Having the brightest colors appear in the foreground of a picture, while having other colors become less distinct with distance.

Converging lines—Receding lines that appear to converge at distant points to show perspective. For examples, look at the receding lines in a long table, up a skyscraper, along a railroad track, or up a stairway.

Detail variation—Placing the clearest detail in the foreground of a picture, while having other details become less distinct with distance.

Eye or station point—The concept that where you are determines your viewpoint.

Foreground, middle ground, background—look at spatial levels.

Foreshortening—A drawing technique showing on object projecting sharply toward or receding from the viewer. Foreshortening creates a visual impact.

Horizon line/eye level line—A perspective term that refers to an imaginary line ahead of you that is level with your horizontal line of sight and on which is located the vanishing point. All edges and lines of the object pictured converge to what is called the vanishing point. Those above eye level recede down to the eye level line and those below eye level converge up to the eye level line.

Overlapping—Partially covering one form with another form. The whole form that is in front of the overlapped form seems closer. Overlapping forms create distance.

Picture plane—The flat, two-dimensional drawing surface on which you create three-dimensional space.

Placement—Placing forms lower in the picture so that they appear to come forward and placing forms higher up in the picture to cause them to appear to recede.

Shading and shadow variation—Using the shading to make objects appear three dimensional.

Size variation—Having the larger forms appear in the foreground of a picture, while having smaller forms recede in the distance.

Spatial levels—Establishing various levels such as the foreground, middle ground, and background to create distance and to indicate which objects are nearest, in between and farthest away.

Developing a Relationship with Art

When teaching art to students and building on their own natural creativity always is thinking of ways to enhance and improve their relationship with the arts. When a lesson has been successful, ask the question how to improve on a good thing, and we usually can.

Thoughts from a Seasoned Artist

In teaching children to draw in class, I did not feel that I could use the methods taught to me in art school. Those methods worked well for the entire student's that were naturally artistic, but as we know not every child that comes into our class room is. The teaching method of Mona Brooks became the method that was used with each of my classes. The method is based on using the five elements of design (circle, dot, straight line, curved line, and angle line) and how these shapes work together to form a picture or an object. Used with children as young as four and adults into their 80's have all been able to learn basic drawing and many have gone on to become really good artist. It is the role of the teacher to seek out and find ideas and products that can help students of all ages become better at the fine art of their choice.

How to Ensure Student Success

One way to ensure that your students gain as much knowledge along with freedom inside your classroom is to develop the characteristics needed to be artistic in your teaching. The following ideas will help add to your success.

1. Become a collaborative teacher and planner; invite in guest artist.
2. Build relationships with your students that develop trust and form a basis for the discipline within your classroom.
3. Continue to learn. Always seek out new ideas to share, methods that are helpful and research anything that is about emerging artist or new styles in art.
4. Become more optimistic about teaching and what you are doing within your classroom. Make your goal one to reach "all" students that can be differentiated using arts-based concepts.
5. Use humor to make yourself more relatable to your students. It will enhance your classroom environment.
6. Be passionate about the arts and speak of all of the arts often in class. Ask questions of your students. Example: Have you heard this song before? Did you see in the paper that a play is coming to our city that has won many awards? Has anyone seen the art done by this artist, what do you think of it? Keep discussion about arts passionate!
7. Ask students go give you ideas with problems (some you might even create yourself). Example: Does anyone know a better way to keep the tops on our glue bottles from getting lost?
8. Become a mentor to your students. Find out their interest and see if it is something you can relate to. Find the common grounds you share. Make yourself approachable.
9. Be brave and show confidence that you are not afraid to make a mistake and ask for help.
10. Develop a style or something you are "known" for that sets you apart. It might be a pair of glasses; or the fact you always wear a tie etc.
11. Be enthusiastic about being with the students at this time in their lives.
12. Become more flexible to changing a schedule, or meeting with students at a different time to take full advantage of those teachable moments.

The classroom is your home, make all that enter into your classroom feel welcome.

CHAPTER 4
Music in the Classroom

Music Is All around Us

Music is an integral part of human life. Take a moment to consider how music impacts your own life. Stop to consider the moments throughout the day that use musical elements that are rarely ever notice. Early in the morning alarm clocks are going off, some with loud beeping sounds tapping out a steady rhythm, others may play music blasting through the silence of the night in an attempt to rouse someone from a deep sleep. Once awake the television may be turned on, blasting music underneath commercials or even a newscast. An example is a recent Amazon.com commercial that features a dog wearing a bright blue cast and the sounds of voices humming a tune as scenes of the dog play out and a young man sees the dog and goes to order a product from Amazon and then a very gruff voice begins singing. The visual images may not be as important as the music in this commercial. The first time the commercial is viewed you may ask why they chose that song to go with that commercial. Hours later you may find yourself humming the tune since it has found a way into your subconscious.

Once you have dressed for the day perhaps, you get into the car and turn the radio on and listen to music as you drive to work. Arriving at work you may walk through a door with an audible alert that announces your entrance with the ringing of a bell, or a "ding, ding." Arriving at your desk you power-up the computer and music begins to play indicating that it is starting. Suddenly your cell phone rings playing a happy tune. Throughout the day, music will surround you and more than likely your conscious mind will dismiss and you will not even be aware that it exists.

An experiment to really understand the importance of music and sound is to watch a movie with the volume muted. Notice that the action is not as vivid, and it may even be difficult to understand the mood that the movie director is trying to portray. A suspenseful scene is much more vivid with the "bah dum, bah dum" of impending doom rather than silence. Try another experiment with a television comedy show. Turn the volume down and see if the comedy is as vivid without the laugh track underneath the action. Although the laugh track is not music, it is similar because it is used to evoke emotion in the viewer just as music is used to underscore the plot and guide the viewer helping them to experience the proper emotion for each developing scene.

As you can see music surrounds us every day of our lives. If music is around us everywhere then why is n't it in our classrooms. Music does not have to be a constant presence in a classroom, but it can provide a rich enhancement to learning from time to time throughout the day in a classroom.

Tarchyshnik Andrei/Shutterstock.com

Creating the Atmosphere for Learning

Establishing an atmosphere that encourages student learning is one of the greatest challenges for a teacher. Early in the morning when students come in still sleepy, and having a difficult time focusing on the work for the day it may help to play a peppy, lively tune to encourage them to wake up. After a trip to physical education or the playground the students may be overactive and hyped up and soothing calm music can often help to calm them down. In addition to calming the students down, calm soothing music is also able to help students to refocus and reset their minds for learning. Music can help ease the burden of the afternoon slump when students return from lunch after eating and get sleepy. Playing a lively tune can help wake the students up and get them moving both physically and mentally.

The atmosphere for learning is very important. Most teachers go to great lengths to create visually stimulating areas within the classroom. A second grade teacher worked for days before school started to provide visual stimulation for her students by creating a huge tree out of paper with branches and leaves dangling from the ceiling above the students' heads. Another area of the same classroom had a reading area with pillows and stuffed animals to provide a tactile environment to encourage student learning. Throughout the day, she would play music to encourage student learning which helped to round out the classroom atmosphere so that all the senses were impacted to encourage learning.

I Can't Sing!!!

A teacher does not have to be musically talented to include music within the classroom. Since music is all around us throughout the day, it makes sense to include it in the classroom learning environment. Each person is born with creativity and if you have not been given the ability to sing then you must employ the creative element that you were born with. Music is a vital element within the classroom and since you can't or won't sing, is it right to remove music completely from the classroom? The availability of music today through a variety of resources can allow you to include music without ever having to sing. However, it must be said that if music is an active part of a classroom even the nonsinging teacher may find themselves singing along from time to time.

Now that we have established that a teacher does not have to sing in the classroom. It should be said that a classroom teacher should sing with their students from time to time. The reason is that the teacher is the model and example for the students. How can a teacher expect the students to be creative and perform if the teacher is afraid to perform for the students? The reality of the situation is that the students are not going to be nearly as critical as adults who have been shown that only the Mariah Carey's of the world should open their mouth and let music come out. Students are very forgiving and are so excited when a teacher wants to lead them in singing and demonstrating the actions through music.

Each person is an artist!

Art is expression!

Music is a form of Art!

Each person has the ability to express themselves with musical sounds. When and how that person chooses to express themselves is the determining factor within their independent artistic journey through life.

Thoughts from a Seasoned Artist

Allowing a student to perform for their peers can open doors for them that might have never been approached before. A third-grade student wanted to perform and play the guitar in a music class one day. The teacher wanting to encourage this creative outlet created a performance time each Friday which allowed students to come and perform. The young third-grade boy eagerly starting to bring his guitar to class on Fridays and played for the class. This simple action by the music teacher created a spark within the boy who went on to take music lessons and develop his talent. As the young boy grew, he developed his talent to the point that he was able to matriculate into the famed Juliard

Thoughts from a Seasoned Artist (*Continued*)

School of Music. Attending Juliard is an accomplishment in itself, but this young man was able to begin study there in the ninth grade as a freshman in high school. The music teacher was not aware of the impact she had on the young man until one day a newspaper headline featured the young man and within the article he was quoted a stating that "his third-grade music teacher inspired him to learn music and encouraged him to succeed." Even the smallest decision a teacher makes can have a lasting impact on a student.

Instrumental or Vocal Music?

Every person should have a basic understanding of music. Music is composed of notes on a staff and uses rhythm and pitch to create musical sounds that are perceived as music by the listener. Musical notes are similar to the alphabet that is used in writing words, except a musical alphabet is limited to seven notes (letters). The musical alphabet begins with the letter "A" and ends with the letter "G." Looking at a piano keyboard you will see a series of seven notes A, B, C, D, E, F, G arranged in a pattern to create 88 keys. An easy way to understand the notes on a piano is to note the location of the black keys. You will notice that there are a series of black keys in groups of two and three keys. The notes associated with the series of two black keys are "C" on the left, "D" between the two black keys, and "E" on the right side of the black keys. The notes associated with the series of three black keys are "F" on the left, followed by "G" and "A" in the middle, and "B" on the right. Now that you have this basic information do you feel equipped to teach music in the classroom? It is not reasonable to expect every classroom teacher to be able to go and find a "C" on a piano keyboard, but it is not difficult for a classroom teacher to have an understanding that the musical alphabet is composed of seven letters representing notes.

Lindwa/Shutterstock.com

Instrumental music is just that it is created using musical instruments and contains no voices singing along with the music. Vocal music uses vocalists to sing the words to the song or to hum along with the music as part of the musical presentation. The difference in these two varieties of musical style are important for the classroom teacher to understand. Instrumental music is great to provide a specific feeling for the classroom environment as students are working on a project or classwork. There is nothing wrong with vocal music, but sometimes the words cause the student to become distracted as they sing along with the words to the song. Therefore, it is extremely important that music in the classroom be selected in an intentional manner to support student learning.

To Rap or not to Rap

Music in the classroom is often interpreted as a rap to describe the solar system or some other subject that the students could be studying. While there is a place for such music by no means should a classroom teacher be limited to just simple action songs that teach elements of a lesson. Using music in creative ways to manipulate the students and direct their learning should be the goal of the classroom teacher. Just as music sets the mood for a scene in a movie it can set the mood in the classroom. Combining music with creative writing is an opportunity to broaden the student's musical horizons while helping to encourage the development of their writing skills. When studying the American Revolution look for classical music of the period and play the selection while the students are doing creative writing. If the class is studying colonial America, the teacher might give a writing prompt such as "write a letter to your parents describing the activities of the Boston Tea Party as if you were an eye witness." While the students are writing the song "Revolutionary Tea" might be playing for inspiration. Another colonial writing prompt might be the lyrics to the song "Father and I Went Down to Camp," which was set to the tune of "Yankee Doodle Dandy."

"Father and I Went Down to Camp"

Father and I went down to camp,
Along with Captain Gooding,
And there we see the men and boys
As thick as hasty pudding.
Chorus:
Yankey doodle keep it up,
Yankey doodle dandy;
Mind the music and the step,
And with the girls be handy.

Project the lyrics to the song on the blackboard and ask the students to interpret what the song means. Encourage them by asking what the composer might have been thinking when they wrote the song. After class discussion invite the students to think about an important event in their own lives and have them write a song about it. Then have the students that share their original songs.

Thoughts from a Music Teacher

While teaching a fifth-grade music class I day one particular child had been a nightmare during the class. Acting up and not paying attention throughout the entire lesson. After the class as the students were leaving the teacher heard the notes of Fur Elise by Beethoven coming from the piano. She was so impressed that she got another teacher to come and listen to the child play the piano. After the student began playing the piano and the music teacher praised him his behavior became much better in class. Hearing the teacher praise him gave the student enough courage and confidence that it not only improved his behavior in music class but also other classes showed an improvement in his grades. Performing in music allowed the student to gain a new focus in all areas of his life through a single success in one area. By the end of the school year, the student had progressed so much that he ended up being the Master of Ceremonies for the student talent show. His success and recognition in music gave him the confidence to be successful in other areas of his life.

Pixel Embargo Andrei/Shutterstock.com

Humans are Hardwired for Music

Children Are Hardwired for Music!

The brain of the student is hardwired for detecting sounds and patterns of sounds. Each human begins life surrounded by the rhythm of the mother's beating heart. In addition to the solid steady rhythm of a heartbeat, other sounds enter the womb as the developing embryo grows. The brain is developing along with the body and interpreting not only the sounds of the heartbeat but also the rhythm of each movement the mother makes. The people the mother encounter demonstrate a variety of pitch and sounds that the baby is interpreting with the developing brain.

Encountering music has the potential to use the whole brain. Music whether read, listened to or played uses cognitive, psychomotor, affective, auditory, and visual centers of the brain. Research has indicated that the entire brain is activated when a musician is playing music.

Musical Feelings

Music is capable of rousing emotion within the musician as well as the listener. Consider songs that you have listened to. Some songs arouse happy feelings while others can bring sadness and even tears. Music can also arouse patriotic feelings. Consider the national anthem. What do you think of when you hear that song? To some, it may bring images of soldiers fighting for the freedom of Americans, others might think of the presentation of the flag at a sporting event. Whatever comes to mind "The Star Spangled Banner" was written to chronicle the history of the United States and the brave men who fought to keep the country free. One line of the song reads "whose broad stripes and bright stars through the perilous fight." Consider that the 13 stripes represent the British colonies who declared independence and fought to create a new nation and the blue field of stars represent each of the states that have joined the Union. Although the importance of the national anthem has been somewhat lessened in recent years through the use at public events such as sporting events all across the nation, it still has the power to evoke emotion. Sporting events are not evil by any means, they just provide numerous opportunities to experience the national anthem and create the possibility of the audience just going through the motions to get the game started rather than actually pausing to consider what the anthem actually represents and the importance of respecting the Flag of the United States of America.

Music Represent the Times

Music reflects the historical time when it was created. World War II was a time when the United States was coming out of the greatest depression in their history. War was not popular, and President Roosevelt was in a difficult place. The war in Europe was raging and the United States was reluctant to get involved. Then on the fateful Sunday morning of December 7, 1941, a vicious attack disabled most of the American Pacific fleet as the ships were anchored at Pearl Harbor, Hawaii. President Roosevelt addressed congress the next day stating "yesterday December 7, 1941 . . . a date which will live in infamy . . . the United States of America was suddenly and deliberately attacked by naval and air forces of the Empire of Japan." He went on to describe the peaceful conditions between the two nations before the attack.

The music of the period quickly adjusted to the mood of the American people and promoted the war effort. Songs such as "Praise the Lord and Pass the Ammunition" by composer

Frank Loesser, rallied the popular notion that God was with the United States as they fought the enemy. One of the most rousing patriotic songs of this period was Irving Berlin's "God Bless America" which aroused intense emotion across the land. Another song that was recorded on December 16, 1941, by Dick Robertson was Goodbye Mama ('m off to Yokohama) written by composer J. Fred Coots, tells the story of Johnny who was a Yankee through and through and heard that his country needed him to go and fight the Japanese. The chorus tells his mama that he is going to Yokohama to inform the Japanese that the Yanks are not going to be bullied.

The war in Europe brought even more music Jimmy Dorsey and his orchestra recorded "(There'll be Bluebirds Over) The White Cliffs of Dover" in 1942, other songs such as "Comin in On a Wing and Prayer" encouraged the soldiers and the American people that God was with them and to keep pressing onward. The songs of World War II were not all about aggression or God protecting the soldiers. The lyrics of the song, "When the Lights Go On Again" are nonaggressive and hopeful of peace returning to the world again. One of the most poignant lines of the song refers to kisses and how they will not represent goodbyes anymore, but Hello's.

RetroClipArt/Shutterstock.com

Music was actually part of the war effort the United States employed to fight World War II. Radio was a key element of a soldier's life and therefore was used to encourage them and reinforce the reason that they were fighting the war. It would be remiss to consider the impact of music on the American people at home while their loved ones were off fighting a war across the Pacific and in Europe. The song "I'll Walk Alone" was recorded by several musical artists, but Dinah Shore first introduced it in Universal Studios film *Follow the Boys (1944)* the film helped to take the song to the top of the music charts. Although most songs were written from the perspective of a soldier "I'll Walk Alone" was written from the point of view of the lover who was left behind at home waiting for the soldier to return. Another popular song during the 1940s was made famous by Glenn Miller and the Andrews sisters. "Don't Sit Under the Apple tree (with Anyone Else but Me)," the melody was composed by Sam H. Stept was based on another song that was based on a nineteenth century English folk song. After the United States entered World War II in 1941, Lew Brown and Charles Tobias adapted lyrics that they had written for a 1939 musical to create the famous wartime version which ends with a line that talks about a soldier coming home from battle. The song was recorded by Glen Miller Orchestra in February 1942 with vocals by Tex Beneke, Marion Hutton, and The Modernaires a few months later the song was featured in the Universal Studios film *Private Buckaroo* which featured the Andrews sisters and permanently linked them to the song becoming one of the most requested songs from the singing trio. "Don't Sit Under the Apple Tree" is significant because it was featured on the radio hit parade with three different recorded versions by different musical artists at the same time.

Music is a natural choice when students are learning about various periods in history. Listening to the music of the time can often reveal a great deal about the culture and the people of the period. Using music in a history lesson helps create memory markers that allow the student to associate the musical sounds with events that were happening during that period of history. The example of World War II can be applied at any time in history. After the attack on the World Trade Center on 2001, music reflected the events and emotion of the American people. Darryl Worley recorded the song "Have You Forgotten?" which featured prominent lines in the song encouraging people to remember how and what they felt on September 11, 2001. Other lines of the song indicate the offensive nature of the images from that day on the television and how they had been removed to protect the viewing public. When planning a history lesson consider the music of the period, as well as the visual and theatrical arts of the period. Fine Arts are a reflection and a statement of the times.

Student Success

The success of students in a classroom is essential in order for students to have the confidence to succeed and advance their learning. Providing opportunities that allow students to succeed no matter how insignificant can foster confidence that can lead to greater student success. A music teacher was instructing her students about musical instruments. It came time in the lesson to teach the students how to play a recorder. This was usually a very exciting time in the year for the teacher, but this time there was a student in the class that was disabled and did not have hands. This particular student had a strong desire to learn to play the recorder, but without fingers, it was doubtful that this could ever happen. The teacher was torn and was not sure how to help the student, for she had never taught someone to play without fingers. After talking with the student and having him hold the recorder she discovered that if tape was placed over one of the holes on the recorder the student was able to cover the remaining holes in order to play notes. After taping the hole and working diligently with the student, the teacher was able to teach the student to play "Hot Cross Buns" on the recorder. Not only did the student learn to play the song, but also he enthusiastically practiced each day. The teacher was amazed at how well he was doing and adapting to overcome the obstacles brought on by the absence of fingers. In fact, he eventually was able to play the recorder better than some of the other students in the class. When it came time for the school talent show he was the first student to sign up and audition. Not only did he perform beautifully in the school talent show, but also he brought tears to the eyes of some of the parents and achieved a pivotal success within his own life. The teacher not only provided a solution for a simple music lesson but also taught the student something much more valuable. The student learned that he could adapt to most situations and successfully accomplish just about anything. The student was very removed from the class before the teacher was able to provide him a way to succeed. The success of playing the recorder made a huge impact on the student. Years later, he credited the music teacher with showing him never to give up and that he could accomplish anything he set out to do.

Music Miracles

Miracles through music happen every day of the year, but one in particular was a phenomenal achievement that was unexpected. The year had started with overloaded classes of 60 students at a time and the music teacher was exhausted when the next class arrived. In this particular, class was a nonverbal student who was not an ideal student for a music classroom since she spent the entire day screaming unexpectedly from time to time. After 2 days in music, the student began to sit still and listen to the songs the other children were singing. The teacher observed this, but did not think much about it, but as time passed the student became calmer and would sit and listen to the words and move to the music. Music spoke to her and allowed a way to express herself physically rather than just screaming.

One day the class was learning a bilingual song and the teacher had shown the class motions to go with the words to the song. The student loved doing the movements and was very expressive dancing and moving as the other students sang. The song was a Spanish song with the words "come over and look at my garden it is beautiful." [song lyrics written by Daryl Worley] The students were instructed to form a half circle to indicate a rainbow for the word beautiful. The student quickly learned the hand motions and one day unexpectedly, she blurted out the word "beautiful" as she created the motions for the rainbow. This moment of success would not have been possible if the teacher had been successful in removing the student the first week of school.

The teacher had requested that the student be removed from the room because she was proving to be a complete disruption and distraction with the constant screaming. By the second week of school, it was obvious that the student had begun to make a connection with the music. The teacher's mind was changed and the student was allowed to stay in the class and eventually after singing the song the student grew to love the music class and would sit quietly and move to the music and actively participate in the class. Eventually, the small success in music was carried over to the student's other classes and allowed her to start the journey toward becoming a verbal communicator as well as a music enthusiast.

retrorocket/Shutterstock.com

Musical Elements

There are seven basic elements of music. Each element comes together to make the entire musical creation richer and fuller sounding to the ear.

1. Melody—sometimes referred to as the tune of a song. Melody is the basic grouping of sounds that create a song.
2. Harmony—accents the melody and creates a pleasing sound to accompany the melody.
3. Rhythm—sets the pace and contains the beat of the music in a variety of patterns and forms according to the length of the notes that are selected.
4. Dynamics—dictates the loudness or softness of music.
5. Texture—reveals the depth and richness of the combination of tones, rhythm, and harmony within the music.
6. Form—represents the outline or skeleton of the music. Form is the basic order of music.
7. Style—refers to the way the music is heard or performed. A Beethoven symphony has a different style than a Lady Gaga hit song.

The elements of music are simple descriptors of the various parts that can be put together to create a musical whole.

Musical Interpretation

A learning disabled student was placed in a music class and was extremely shy and introverted. The teacher was amazed that when it was time to sign up for the talent show her name was on the list. When the teacher asked what her talent was the student said that she was an artist. The teacher was reluctant to let the student perform as an artist so he began to probe for a little more information from the student. It was decided that the student would demonstrate her talent for the teacher the next day. The teacher was reluctant, but he agreed and the next day she came in with a large drawing pad and an easel and a musical CD. The teacher really did not know what to expect as the student was very ordinary and did nothing to stand out and make an impression of any kind. As the music started the student took out a paint brush and began to paint on the canvas. Her movements were exquisitely produced to match the emotion of the music. The teacher was enthralled as he watched the amazing display in front of him. Not only was the student moving and expressing the music physically, but also she was creating a beautiful artistic expression on the canvas. The teacher was so moved that he applauded loudly and told the student what a beautiful talent she had demonstrated. At the talent show, the audience was filled with over one thousand parents and students who watched in awe as the student interpreted the music through movement and the expression of a paint brush across the canvas. The audience was very moved by the experience and applauded loudly for the young student. The student ended up winning third place in the talent show for creating an artwork while music played. In that moment, the student's disability did not exist but had been replaced with the joy of artistic expression. The reality of the moment demonstrated that a shy student with a disability who blended into the crowd in the classroom blossomed like a rose when encouraged by the feeling and emotion she felt from a connection to music. This connection allowed her to express herself freely with a paintbrush and a canvas.

The Vocabulary of Music

A cappella	vocal singing without instrumental accompaniment
Articulation	the process of how a note is started or ended
Attack	the origin or beginning of a sound
Chord	three or more notes played at the same time
Counting	the division or breakdown of rhythm into beats of time
Crescendo	when music becomes gradually louder
Diction	the correct and clear pronunciation of consonants
Dynamics	the loudness or softness of music
Forte	loud

Harmony	when notes or chords come together to make a blended sound
Improvisation	creating music without a written musical plan. Making it up as you play
Melody	a sequence of pitches that form a pattern
Note	a symbol used to notate the duration and pitch of a musical sound
Piano	soft
Phrase	a group of notes sung or played together as one musical thought
Pitch	a measure of high and low sounds
Pulse	feeling of the rhythm or beat, the heartbeat of a musical piece
Rhythm	the placement of notes and sounds in a pattern
Score	music notated and written down in order to show all of the parts for each instrument or voice
Sotto voce	quietly
Staccato	notes played or sung sharply and crisply
Stanza	the verse of a song
Tempo	the speed of music
Timbre	the darkness or brightness of a sound

CHAPTER 5
Theatre in the Classroom

The terms Theatre and Drama are used interchangeably many times; however, it is important to establish the difference since most classrooms who integrate the arts will be using drama rather than theatre. Drama is the informal study or presentation of the performing arts. Theatre is the formal study or presentation of the performing arts. Most children begin to dabble in drama at a very early age as they act out various scenarios in the form of play. An example would be a group of young children playing "cops and robbers." One child may pretend to be the robber while the other child pretends to be the cop who is chasing him.

arbit/Shutterstock.com

Dramatic play in children helps them to interpret experiences and events in order to better understand them. Although this is a subconscious activity it is similar to a dream sequence during sleep patterns where the brain is sorting out various data and cataloguing it into a logical order. Imagine yourself after viewing a movie. The events of the movie have taken you on a roller coaster ride of emotions resulting in a sense of closure and peace at the end of the movie for the main character. This in turn causes you to feel an uplift of emotion and happiness as you leave the theater. The Greeks called this catharsis or a purging or cleansing

47

of the soul. The ability to manipulate the emotions of an audience demonstrates the power that performing arts can have on an audience.

Dramatic play in a learning environment is a tool that can create memory markers that will bring the material of the lesson to life for the student. The Catholic Church in the middle ages discovered that acting out Bible stories was an effective tool to teach the illiterate populations of the period. Since the majority of the population was not able to read and the mass was delivered in Latin, a language the people did not speak, much less understand, knowledge of Bible stories was primarily passed down to each generation from the previous generation. Works of art within the cathedrals served to remind the people of the various stories in the Bible. Intricate carved statues or a painting on the ceiling, such as Michelangelo's famous painting in the Sistine Chapel that depicted the creation of Adam created a visual reminder of the verbal stories the parishioners had heard from birth. Statues were used to create a life-sized version of the nativity story that was used to celebrate the birth of Jesus. These life size statues eventually gave way to live actors who acted out roles of each character resulting in a rise of dramatic story telling as part of the mass. The plays within the church became so popular that church officials were concerned that the focus was shifting away from God and they forced the performances outside of the walls of the church.

Dramatic play allows students to explore without the fear of failure. Young minds are filled with creative thoughts. It is much easier for a kindergartner to demonstrate creativity than a sixth grader. The rules and restrictions imposed on students by classroom teachers and school officials many times discourages creative thoughts and expression resulting in students who are afraid to be creative. A kindergarten parent was amazed to learn that the children were not allowed to speak at lunch. The Principal of the school boasted with pride that the lunchroom was so quiet you could hear a pin drop. This statement was very disturbing to the parent who had observed a change of behavior in her young son. Before he had started to school, he was a happy child who would sing and play with his friends. Now he was withdrawn and quiet and would hardly speak. When he did speak, it was with anger and frustration. As the parent talked with her young son she discovered that the Principal had publicly reprimanded her son during lunch because he offered to share his apple with a friend. Upon further investigation, it was brought to her attention that the Principal stood at the front of the lunchroom with a microphone which caused her to have a booming threatening voice when she reprimanded the students. The students associated lunchtime as a very negative experience rather than a time to share and express themselves with each other. As the parent investigated further, she discovered that the students were allowed 15 min a day to speak freely and express themselves during recess. At all other times, they were to sit quietly and speak only when they were asked to do so. The inability to express himself was creating a child who was increasingly angry and lashing out at others. Humans have a need to communicate and children should be allowed to communicate freely in a variety of forms.

Storytelling

Humans have been communicating by telling stories since the beginning of time. Storytelling has played a very important part in recording historical information through the ages. The Bible instructs the children of Israel to pass key information down to each generation so that they would not grow up unaware of their heritage. Since the world populations were primarily illiterate until the invention of the printing press, oral history was a key element in communicating family heritage from one generation to the next.

Lorelyn Medina/Shutterstock.com

Children are natural storytellers and tapping into this ability can encourage them to develop not only creative thinking abilities but excellent writing skills as well. Setting aside 5 min each day that are dedicated to creative writing and storytelling can create an incredibly large impact on a student's ability to express themselves. The activities should be varied each day to promote original thought and develop a variety of forms of expression.

Sample Creative Writing Plan

Monday	Simple writing prompt (It was a bright sunny morning in the forest as Chip scurried around gathering . . .)
Tuesday	Five words to include in a story (Happy, Laughter, Cake, Blue, Surprise)

Sample Creative Writing Plan (*Continued*)

Wednesday	Storytelling exercise (Stand four students shoulder to shoulder at the front of the class. The teacher should stand behind the row of students and instruct them that a story prompt will be given and when they are tapped on the back they are to immediately start speaking and complete the thought and keep the story going until they are tapped again. The teacher should tap one student indicating they should stop speaking and simultaneously tap another student to indicate that they should continue the thought.)
Thursday	Concise thoughts (Ask students to write a sentence in 10 words or less that describes the plot of their favorite movie. After they have completed the sentence ask them to edit the sentence to three words.)
Friday	Free writing (Students are to write about something that happened to them during the past week.)

Encouraging the expansion of students' minds can take only minutes a day but can provide an incredible advantage in relation to student performance in the classroom. The example provides five suggestions for a variety of prompts to encourage student interaction. These activities encourage creative thinking and expression. Another great activity for creative expression uses music and art to allow the student to express feelings on paper while listening to music. This simple exercise can then be expanded to allow the students to creatively move to the music and physically interpret the drawing they created.

The example for Tuesday presented five words to include in a story. These words can be anything that encourages creative thought. Including current spelling or vocabulary words can be very beneficial but be careful when selecting the words. If all five words are difficult, it can cause the student to be cautious when writing. Using two to three vocabulary words with two action words helps prevent creative blockages for students.

The example for Thursday is an easy tool to help students learn to summarize and find the main thoughts in a sentence. If students were asked to summarize their favorite movie in three words they might be completely at a loss where to start. Allowing them to write a sentence that describes the movie demonstrates narrowing down the information to a more manageable size. After they have completed the ten word sentence it is much easier to choose three words to restate the thought in the sentence.

The example for Friday encourages students to express themselves about any topic that they choose. It also allows a glimpse into the lives of the students and any problems that might be present that the teacher might not know exist. The student's privacy should be very important to encourage pure thoughts in the writing. It is extremely important that these thoughts be guarded and not shared with the entire class unless the student gives permission.

An easy way to keep all the student's creative writing endeavors together in one place is to have students obtain a spiral notebook that will serve as their personal writing journal. Depending on the age of the student, this can be used to instruct them on following a particular format (the date must be in the upper right corner). When grading these assignments, it is important to consider using a completion grade rather than a critical examination of what the student has written. When students are aware that their work will be critically analyzed, it inhibits the creative process. The goal should be to allow the students complete freedom of expression without retaliation through grading.

Rawpixel/Shutterstock.com

Human beings naturally select roles to play each day of their lives. Researchers have discovered that the birth order of children has an impact on the role they have within a family unit. Consider a group project you might have worked on with other people. Did every person assume the role of the leader? Most likely that was not the case since many leaders in a group can result in complete chaos. A trained actor studies the various roles that people assume and mimics particular traits that are exhibited in order to give the impression of a character. In the classroom, the roles students choose to portray have the potential to be just as intricately interpreted as a role portrayed by a professional actor. The key difference is that the roles that a student might choose will most likely be based on known stereotypes about the character they are going to portray.

Encouraging students to act out roles or participate in role play sometimes requires some coaching. Creative role play requires input from the student who is creating the role; however, a few basic ideas can help spur the creative spirit within the student. An example would be a teacher who is going to take the students in his class on a walk through the forest. This walk is not a traditional hike through a forest. Instead, the teacher instructs the students that they are going to create a forest within the classroom. He then asks the students to list things that might be in the forest. As the students list each thing the teacher writes them on the board so that the students can see them. After a short brainstorming session the students are asked to choose one of the items listed to portray in the classroom forest.

Since drama combines all the arts, at this point, the teacher could instruct the students to draw a picture of the character they have chosen to portray. After each student has created a visual image, then they could be prompted to create a costume element to wear or a prop to use while portraying the character. An example might be cutting several leaves and taping them to the student's shirt if they were portraying a tree. A child portraying a squirrel might need a large seed or nut to use as a prop to help them demonstrate what a squirrel might do in the forest. After the students have created a costume element or prop to aide them in portraying the role, they have chosen they are ready to explore the forest. The teacher has chosen a classical piece of music to play while the students portray their characters. The students are encouraged to listen and feel the power of the music and move with the music.

This example is a very basic idea of portraying a character within the classroom. Older students can get into portraying characters just as much as a young child. The type of character becomes more intricate as the student ages. For instance, a High School student could easily engage in a simulation activity that allows them to own a fantasy football team. Owning a fantasy football team may not be very practical in a classroom setting, but recreating a moment in history or acting out a student's interpretation of a character's life before they enter the story in the pages of a novel serves a distinct purpose in a secondary classroom.

In order to equip a student to portray a character it is helpful to provide them with the tools to be successful. A character profile worksheet is composed of several questions that reveal things about the life of the character, such as the type of work they might do or where they live and what they eat. The character profile worksheets can be adapted to specific objectives that fit the individual lesson. A professional actor would complete a character profile in order to better understand the character and develop the tools necessary to portray the character.

Encouraging an elementary student to portray a character should be based on the stereotypes that the student perceives about the character. For instance, if a student was going to portray a lion they more than likely would consider the lion's roar as a key characteristic for portrayal of the animal. Another obvious characteristic is the fact that a lion walks on four legs so the student will naturally want to crawl on their hands and knees to imitate the lion. As students grow and learn and explore creatively they eventually will explore the possibilities of creating a character that is not completely composed of stereotypes.

Imitation or Interpretation

When students begin to interpret a role they tend to rely heavily on imitation to create the character. Just as a young baby begins imitating things that it has heard in order to learn to speak, a student must begin with imitation in order to grasp an understanding of how to portray a character. A first grader must rely heavily on stereotypical ideas in order to portray a character, whether it is an object, animal, or human being. In contrast, a sixth grader might still rely on stereotypes in order to gather initial ideas, but as they begin to develop and interpret those same ideas they will begin to create a unique idea that may go against the initial stereotype.

In order to interpret a role, a student must be encouraged to freely express themselves without fear of failure. An example in the visual art world might be a dog stepping in paint and walking across a canvas. This might be viewed as artwork, but was it intentional art or accidental? An artist intentionally places paint on a canvas in order to express an idea. A student who is asked to recreate a person from history must research not only the person, but also historical event and lifestyles from the period that the person lived. After they have completed the research, then they are able to interpret the material and bring a representation of the person to life. In contrast, a young elementary student might be asked to portray a wolf in a classroom play. The student has a good idea what a wolf is like so very little research is required to fulfill the portrayal of a wolf.

Interpretation

Music can provide a great backdrop in the classroom to encourage creative movement with students. It is very important to consider that each child is going to interpret movement in a unique and individual way. An example would be children hopping like bunnies. Some might squat on all four and hop with their legs and use their hands to help them balance. Others could squat down in an upright position with their arms against their sides, elbows bent and hands at the chest level (almost like a puppy dog looks when it sits up), hopping in an up and down motion in place rather than around the room. Although each of these children interpreted the movement of a bunny they approached it in different ways.

vita khorzhevska/Shutterstock.com

If a rubric had been assigned to this project, it could have interfered with the creativity of the student. For example, when a teacher creates a rubric, they traditionally have a single approach to solving the assignment which does not allow room for a creative response from the student. If the teacher had stipulated in the rubric that the student must hop like a rabbit on all fours, the student who hopped vertically would be marked down because they were not on all fours. Also, if the rubric was presented before the students created the movement of the bunnies every student would be on all fours since the rubric called for that action. This takes the creativity out of the assignment because the movement was suggested within the rubric.

Creative Assignments and Rubrics

Rubrics are not completely bad. Creative assignments can maintain the creative potential if a **blind rubric** is used. Blind rubrics are created by the teacher to aid in grading the assignment, but not shared with the student. Working with creativity in students requires a very positive atmosphere with limited ability to fail if the student attempts something. Therefore, a critique of a creative performance should not be critical of choices the student has made, but rather focus on execution of the assignment.

Consider the assignment to hop like a bunny. The two students described in the example both executed their interpretation of the bunny resulting in accomplishing the given task. If the teacher had added another direction such as hop like a bunny and move across the room and eat a carrot then the potential for a mistake is increased. Student A dropped down on all fours and hopped across the room and bent down and pretended to eat the carrot from the ground (floor). Student B hopped vertically about four feet and then stopped and like Bugs Bunny reached out and grabbed an imaginary carrot and began chewing on it. Both students interpreted the assignment, however Student B moved only four feet. Does this indicate that this student followed directions completely? To assess this more background information is needed. The teacher had just completed a vocabulary lesson that included the words hop, across, and carrot. During this particular lesson he had indicated through a demonstration that across the room was from one side of the room to the other side of the room. Since Student B did not hop completely across the room from one side to the other then a deduction could be made from the score on the assignment.

Hopping like a bunny might have been interpreted differently if the definition of across was not clear to the student. Both Student A and Student B would have been correct since they both moved and hopped and ate the carrot. It is very important for a teacher to consider how much they are projecting the outcome of an assignment when grading. Many times a teacher who sees a totally unique approach to the solution to an assignment realizes that they would never have considered that approach. It is key that the teacher in that situation considers the viewpoint of the student who made that decision before reacting as if it was wrong to make that assumption.

Each student brings the knowledge they have gathered to that particular point in their life into the classroom. This knowledge base is all that they have to assess and interpret any given situation they encounter. Since everyone has a unique personal experience, then their approach to interpreting a situation will be just as unique as their individual background. Just as the two students approached hopping like a bunny in different ways. Student A hopped on all fours, because previously they had seen a live bunny that was close to the ground and moved using all four legs. Student B had never seen a live bunny and relied on the memory of seeing a Looney Tunes cartoon with Bugs Bunny who did n't really hop, but walked and used his front paws like hands. The teacher was not aware of each student's background, but it is clear that personal knowledge affects the creative outcome.

Creative Drama

Creative drama is defined as an improvisational activity that explores human nature using a process oriented activity that is guided by a leader. The role of the leader is to guide the students through the experiences encouraging them to explore, examine and express themselves creatively. A particular benefit from creative drama exercises is the potential to develop problem solving skills. Dramatic exercises encourage students to hypothesize and analyze conflict. As the students begin testing the hypothesis they analyze various outcomes and discover solutions to problems. Each student has the potential to use creative problem solving. Whether or not a student uses creative problem solving is directly related to the amount of negative feedback the student encounters in relation to past creative attempts. Negativity greatly impacts a student's ability to be creative.

Drama provides an essential style of learning since it is closely related to the natural learning process preschoolers used to learn. Preschoolers imitate life in their play "rehearsing" for life. This imitation allows the preschooler to practice a variety of observations that have been made in order to prepare that child for the possibility of actually performing the action as an adult. An example might be a young child playing house, cooking a meal in a pretend kitchen. The child has observed an adult preparing meals and imitates them even to the point of serving a pretend meal to another person.

Drama allows a child to escape and explore areas of life that might not be possible. A young 5-year-old boy was playing one afternoon using a road map. As he played he was pretending that the family was traveling to different places. When it came time to eat lunch his mother called him to eat. He insisted that he had stopped for lunch on his trip, going as far to state the city and his favorite restaurant there. In addition to stopping for lunch, the family had picked up his cousin and they were traveling together on the trip. As hard as the mother tried to convince her son to eat, she could not get him to sit down at the table. He insisted that he had already eaten and was not hungry. This example is an actual event that demonstrates the power of the imagination. The young boy did not eat anything until dinner time after he had returned from his trip with his cousin.

Many creative children also have imaginary friends. Creative dramatics is a guided form of this type of creative activity. Children can easily imagine traveling far away creating a forest and a brook in their minds with the greatest of ease. Adults have a more difficult time suspending their association with reality because they have been criticized and discouraged from using creative abilities. Supporting creativity depends upon taking extreme care not to discourage the creative thoughts by critiquing them. Creativity thrives when encouraged through positive thoughts and positive comments. Creativity can be viewed just as the innocence of a child. Once the innocence is broken it is difficult to go back. Creativity is the same way. Once a creative thought has been criticized it is makes it very difficult to gather the courage to risk failure in the future.

Unlike rehearsing a part for a play, creative drama encourages children to learn to use the talents and skills that they presently possess. The focus of creative drama is not on the memorization of the lines of a play, or intricate blocking (stage directions) for a public performance. Creative drama focuses on exploration and improvisation. The leader of the group discusses a scenario with the students allowing them to internalize ideas then encourages them to act out what was just discussed. This process allows the student to absorb key information and then artistically express the understanding of the new gained knowledge. As creative drama progresses the student is exposed to several theatrical ideas such as exploring character, plot, and most important conflict. Conflict is what drives drama. Without conflict theatre and drama would be static and boring.

Brenna, a 5-year old kept a secret from everyone in her world except for her dearest friend, Poppy the penguin. One day she decided to share her secret with her classmates at school during show and tell. Brenna carefully packed Poppy in her backpack that morning in eager preparation for show and tell time. With each passing moment her excitement was building, when finally her teacher asked the students to come and sit in a circle for show and tell. Brenna was the first one to sit on the rug. She had taken great care to hide Poppy so that the other students could not see him. After everyone was seated it finally became Brenna's turn to present. She pulled Poppy out and proclaimed, "this is Poppy and he has magical powers, we go on trips together all over the world." The students were all very interested in Poppy and his magical powers and began to ask questions about some of the trips. Suddenly one student interjected "can he take us on a trip today?" The teacher quickly recognized an opportunity and stated, "What a great idea, where would you like to go?" Another student quickly said, "let's go on a jungle safari!" The teacher encouraged Brenna to demonstrate how Poppy's magical powers worked. Brenna was so excited that she jumped up holding Poppy and quickly explained that Poppy told her that there was a magical door at the edge of the carpet. Brenna stepped forward and then dropped to her knees proclaiming it is a small door just the right size for Poppy. All the students followed her on their hands and knees as Brenna reached the door and opened it leading the way. Suddenly Brenna stood up and was very excited. "Look over there it is a waterfall!". . . "I see an eagle" . . . another student said, "I see a giraffe." As the creative journey progressed the teacher would direct and encourage the students along their journey. Eventually, the teacher saw an opportunity

(Continued)

to introduce the story that she was planning to read, *Brown Bear, Brown Bear, What do you see?* By Bill Martin, Jr. and Eric Carle. The teacher instructed the students to come and gather round by the waterfall to listen to the story. After the story the teacher instructed the students that it was time for Poppy to take them back to the classroom.

After returning to the classroom the children discussed their journey and the teacher asked them to create a drawing that could serve as a souvenir of their trip that day. The drawings were very diverse, but all seemed to have a common element, Poppy the penguin was in most of them. The imagination of children is so committed that they had no problem imagining that Poppy was traveling with them to view the jungle. The next day the teacher invited the student to act out the story that she had read to them the day before. The teacher played the brown bear and the students pretended to be the other elements of the story.

All children are capable of creating an expression. They are able to create with words, paint, crayons, or even their bodies. The younger the children, the more bold their expressions will be. They are able to create with total freedom even though what they are creating may be perceived as crude. Children are expressive, some of them will grow to be artists one day, but most will enjoy creativity within their childhood before it is cruelly taken away in order for them to comply to the ideas of uniformity and test taking.

Understanding Drama and Theatre

To understand drama it is important to consider the components that form the foundation of theatre and drama. The most basic form of theatre requires two things, a performer and an audience. The performer communicates ideas to the person who is watching them. This is the very basic definition of drama or theatre.

Pavel L Photo and Video/Shutterstock.com

A play is drama that has been organized into three key areas setting, character, and a plot line. The basis of a play is the plot which is developed through the story that is told within the play. Telling the story involves characters who are placed in a specific setting. The beginning of a play introduces the characters and provides the audience with the necessary background information such as setting and the situation and the precursory information needed to understand the conflict that the characters must endure in order to restore a peaceful order. After the background information has been provided to the audience the middle of the play presents the conflict and then the struggle ensues for the characters trying to avoid catastrophe and restore order. The ending of the play brings a resolution to the conflict and restores order in the lives of the characters.

Creative Drama allows students to loosely explore plot, characters, and settings at their own pace. In order for students to grow and progress creatively, they should be encouraged to enact a variety of stories using characters who are in varied situations dealing with multiple types of conflicts. Students should also be encouraged to develop their own unique plots and stories. In order for students to engage in dramatic play, they need to understand a few key concepts.

Conflict

Conflict can be divided into five specific categories, nature, society, relationships, technology, and individual. Conflict involving nature is a broad category. Rain, tornadoes, and earthquakes are just a few examples of natural conflicts that a character might find themselves in. Conflict involving society can be demonstrated by a character such as a maid who manages to overcome the social stigmatism of position in order to become the manager of the hotel where they work. Conflict in relationships are indicated with personal conflict that focuses on the struggle between two characters, such as Cinderella and the wicked stepmother. Conflict with technology involves the interaction of humans with machines. An example might be a family traveling across the desert and their car has overheated, stranding them without water and a way out of the desert. The most critical conflict is often found within the character themselves. Individual conflict is the internal struggle that a character must endure such as the character Pinocchio who longs to be a boy, but is constantly confronted with his personal internal weakness that stand in the way of achieving his goal.

Movement

Interpreting character involves the actions and movement of the characters. When using creative drama it is important to encourage movement that is creative. A student in an introductory acting class may be asked to lay on the floor and pretend to sizzle like bacon in a pan. Although this sounds unusual, it is the same approach that should be taken within the classroom. A young student that is studying the seasons might be asked to be a seed planted in the ground that with the warmth of spring bursts forth and grows into a tree that sways in the summer breeze. The teacher would then instruct the student that the seasons are changing again and asks the students to pretend they are the leaves of the tree blowing to the ground. It is important to consider that the younger the student the more willing to pretend they will be. As children grow they lose creativity as they are criticized and made to feel ashamed of original thoughts and ideas.

The classroom should be a safe haven for original thought rather than a slaughter house that sacrifices the unique abilities of a student in order to create a factory line of cloned students who all function exactly the same. Each student is born with a unique purpose and potential. The integrated arts classroom should encourage the growth of each student guiding them to fulfill their individual potential. Creative movement is a very vulnerable activity for students as they grow older. Establishing a safe zone in the classroom is vitally important when asking a student to expose their original creative thoughts, ideas, and movements.

The idea of a safe zone prepares students to be creative by establishing basic rules that will be followed by each student. The primary emphasis should be removal of all critical remarks and encouraging positive comments and behaviors about each performance. Each participant should feel comfortable without any need to defend themselves or their unique ideas. Critical remarks can destroy creativity and make it very difficult for a student to feel free to express themselves for a very long time after hearing or experiencing the remarks.

Kiselev Andrey Valerevich/Shutterstock.com

Pantomime

Actions without words or pantomime is a very basic form of artistic theatrical expression. Pantomime or mime uses the body of the performer to express a story through the use of movement and physical expression. Young children adapt to the use of pantomime readily. An example of a pantomime activity is a teacher taking the class on an imaginary walk through the forest. Rather than just pretend to hike through the forest the teacher instructs the student to pretend that they are trees, rocks and forest creatures that the teacher can interact with on the walk through the forest. The students pretending to be trees might bend with the wind or wave their branches (arms) in the breeze. The rabbit might hop around on all fours sniffing for a carrot while a squirrel searches for nuts. Young children do not question the idea that they can pretend to be anything.

Creativity is very active in children, but unfortunately by the end of the second grade man schools manage to eliminate most creative thoughts from the minds of children. This is accomplished by endless worksheet and mindless activities that encourage the development of mechanical skills that do not require creative thought. As children grow older their ability to let go and act in a creative manner may diminish, but with careful coaxing can be brought back to life by encouraging original thinking and thought provoking lessons within the classroom. Mime is a favorite activity for older students. They will mime the action of playing an "air" guitar or drinking something from glass.

A great exercise to teach concentration and get the students to focus is the mirror exercise, where two students face each other and one student initiates an action and the other tries to mimic them as though they are staring into a mirror. Students enjoy doing this exercise and it helps with eye and hand coordination as well as concentration. After the students have worked together with mirror exercises change it up a little and have the initiator choose a character such as Cinderella's wicked stepsister preparing to meet the prince. The initiator primps and acts like the character and the student who is mimic the actions serves as the mirror. Allow the students to change roles and act out different characters.

A great activity to help teach vocabulary words is an activity called *Words in Action* where the students watch one student who tries to act out a vocabulary word without speaking. Not only does this activity encourage the making of memory markers, but also it proves to be a fun way for students to engage with their studies while developing their physical interpretation skills. The ability to express oneself without words is priceless and can serve students for the rest of their lives.

A fun pantomime activity is *Night at the Museum*. Students are asked to create a frozen scene in history, such as the signing of the Declaration of Independence. The students form the tableau and stay frozen until given the signal that the moon is rising and it is time to come to life. Based on the popular movie, the students are representing a moment in history as a statue and through the magic of the moonlight they are able to come to life and act out the scene, however there is one catch. The moonlight has allowed them to move, but they are not able to speak.

The Art of the Story

The art of storytelling has been around as long as man has been able to communicate. If a story is told well it can transport the listener to another place and time introducing them to enchanting characters and the struggles and triumphs of their lives. Storytelling throughout history has been used to pass the historical information from one generation to the next in many cultures around the world. This is known as the **oral tradition** which documented the lives and history of a people. The Old Testament in the Bible is composed of oral traditions that have been translated to the written word. The various stories in the Bible are great examples of storytelling.

Telling a story is one of the most basic ways to communicate and allows a student to organize and make sense of things that have or are happening to them in life. Stories do not always have to be spoken to be effective, a written story has just as powerful an impact as a verbal story. When using verbal storytelling in the classroom it is important to stress to the student listeners to pay close attention to what they are hearing. Encouraging the listeners to visualize the story as it is being told is an excellent way to stimulate their minds. After the story is told ask the students to draw a picture that illustrates what the story meant to them. It is important to note that when conducting an exercise such as this there really is no wrong answer to this assignment. When a student is asked to express what something means to them, as long as an effort has been made the assignment should be considered appropriate and complete.

An attempt to define storytelling might include words such as colorful, imaginative, narrative, or even magical. Stories represent exercise for the creative mind building imagination and literary skills. The more practice a student has the better their literary skills will become. Encouraging students to keep a journal allow them to think about what is happening in their lives and to put the events into words to create a story. Journal writing three times a week will work wonders to develop literacy skills. Keeping a journal also provides a reference for students when asked to do exercises that may include writing a story.

As parents and teachers, it is obvious the power that reading a story to young children has in encouraging them to develop communicative skills. The written word has the ability to create a sense of magic that sweeps the reader or listener away to a land of fantasy that can become very real. The event of a story have the power to teach and change the way that things appear and hold the power to be a successful teaching tool. Reading is often emphasized during the education of a child, but it is just as important for the child to learn to tell a story verbally. Developing verbal skills is important because it reinforces verbal communication and discourages stage fright.

Reading a story aloud from a book encourages not only the reader, but also the audience as well to focus completely on the book. When a child is reading a book they visualize the world of the book in their head and completely rely on the words on the page to develop the images. If the book has pictures they serve as signposts that direct the visual images for the reader. As the ability of the reader improves there are fewer pictures which forces the reader to imagine the world of the story in their mind. It is important to note that even though the reader is creating visual images they do not impact the development of the story at all. The story is written in the book and never changes.

Verbal storytelling allows the storyteller to adjust the story to the audience that is listening. Many times if an audience is reacting with laughter and is completely engaged, the storyteller will embellish the story a little in order to heighten the entertainment of their audience. The storyteller uses a narrative format that communicates and encourages a mental imagery in the minds of the audience who is listening to the story. The combination of the storyteller and the audience creates a visual imagery that brings the story to life. It is important to note at this point that audiences use all of their previous experiences to evaluate what they are seeing or hearing. If the storyteller mentions a chair the audience will visualize a chair according to what they perceive to be a chair. Some may picture a wooden chair while others may picture an elaborately upholstered wing chair with gold embellishments.

Imagination and visual creation are valuable and powerful teaching tools in the classroom which empower the reader to analyze and decode words to give them meaning. This visualization is a key to literacy and as a teacher acquiring the skills to integrate artistic expression into the classroom opens the door for students to achieve greater heights in learning. An example of this is an exercise which instructs the student to read a story then summarize it in their own words and then verbally share the story with an audience. Reading the story, analyzing and then evaluating in order to retell the story increases the opportunity to create a memory marker with the lesson. Repetition is a learning tool and the act of reading, analyzing, and retelling allows the student to interact with the material in three distinct ways.

Verbal storytelling provides another venue to expression for students who may not be able to read or write well. Chances are they are able to speak and communicate and idea. Developing verbal storytelling skills encourages the student while developing key knowledge of the structure of language and how it should sound which can be helpful when the student attempts to write a proper sentence.

Every person has a story to tell. Each student in a classroom comes from a different world of experience. Allowing them to analyze and process who they are and where they come from not only helps to build self-confidence, but also encourages other students to move beyond the realm of what they have experienced and empathize with the other situations around them. An example might be a young child who has grown up in a city and is only aware of things that can be found in a city. The student that sits next to them in the class might have been raised on a farm in the country. If each student is allowed to share personal stories with each other there is a potential to create an understanding and to develop a sense of individual pride while encouraging acceptance of others and their situations.

The idea that a story must be memorized in order to tell it should never get in the way of a storyteller. An example might be the fairy tale *Cinderella*. If the story has been heard at least one time then it can be retold by the person who heard it. It is important to note that every event of the story does not have to be told as long as the key events have been covered. This process is made even easier if the listener has visualized the story. Fortunately, for most people in this day and age Walt Disney has created a visual image for Cinderella that strangely enough overpowers any other version of the story. When Disney created the cartoon for Cinderella, several versions of the story were evaluated. The final result was a unique creation from Walt Disney that involved mice and a cat.

Sharing stories creates a sense of community within the classroom. Students are often eager to share what has happened to them. In order to encourage students to share stories, remind them before a holiday to keep a journal of activities so that the entire class can share the holiday with them when they return. Upon returning from a holiday, a fun learning exercise might be a verbal quilt. The verbal quilt is created with images the students draw to share their personal experience to be displayed in the classroom. Once the image has been created then each student presents their image and adds it to the wall to create a visual quilt while at the same time creating a verbal quilt by telling the story to their classmates. The visual images serve as a reminder to the class of the story that it represents.

It is possible for anyone to become a good storyteller. The key to successful storytelling is practice. The best way to start telling stories is to tell a personal story about something that happened to them or their family. The important feature of personal stories is that there is no wrong or right way to tell a story since it is a personal reflection.

Story Prompts:

1. Remember a time when you laughed really hard.
2. What was it like when you learned to ride a bike?
3. Remember your favorite gift.
4. What is your favorite holiday?
5. What makes you happy?

Providing these prompts allows the student to recall events that may have happened to them. If the students are having difficulty coming up with a story then refer to a fairy tale or another story they are familiar with. The children's book series *Little House on the Prairie* by Laura Ingalls Wilder, features stories told by the character Pa throughout the books. If the students have read one of these books have them relate one of Pa's stories in their own words.

Taking a story and personalizing it is important. Just as Walt Disney took the basic story of Cinderella and created his own version to make the cartoon. For example, in one version of Cinderella the step-sisters eyes are plucked out and they cut off their toes to fit into the glass slipper. These elements do not appear in Walt Disney's version of the story. When creating a story consider key qualities that help to identify the characters and look for humor and play it up within the story. It is also important to remember to establish the setting of the story for the audience. This will help them to imagine and visualize what is happening within the story as it unfolds. When adapting a story always stay true to the original message of the story. Avoid the temptation to allow the embellishments of the story to take on a life of their own.

Encouraging creative writing can be a useful tool for developing the skills of storytelling. If the class is keeping a written journal consider providing a written prompt for the story. Providing a prompt should be an occasional activity in order to maintain the creative nature of the assignment. A sample prompt might be "Tommy the squirrel grabbed the nut and . . .," this allows the student to elaborate on the idea of a common character. The variety of stories that can be told from this prompt are endless.

Bringing a Story to Life

After a story has been written on a paper it has an active life in the imagination of the reader, but it also has the potential to come to life for an audience of several people rather than a single reader. When helping students bring a story to life with action, dialogue, and props it is important to allow them considerable freedom in the process of developing a play. The first action required to develop a play from a story is to read the story and create a list of the most important moments within the story.

For example, the fairy tale *Jack and the Beanstalk* can be broken down into scenes to develop into a play. The first scene in the story takes place at Jack's house when a salesman comes to call. The action of the scene involves Jack selling his cow to the man for a sack of beans. Encourage the students to think about this transaction and how they imagine it played out. Then have them improvise the actions of the scenes without words. This will allow them to focus on the action of the scene without words. After they have a grasp for the action within the scene add dialogue to the scene. Explain that dialogue is what drives the story forward by explaining what is happening. The next scene might be the mother scolding Jack for selling the cow for some beans following by the Jack's visit to the home of the giant. Encouraging the students to create an outline of the scenes will help them to organize the action of the play in a useful way.

Creating the play is similar to building a house. The foundation is made up of the scenes that makeup the story of the play. Upon the foundation is the dialogue creating the walls which help to move the story forward. Resting on the walls is the action of the play which forms the roof of the house. Combining the order of the scenes with dialogue and action creates the framework for the play.

Once the play is created the audience should be considered. Will the play be presented for peers within the classroom or possibly parents? Once the audience is determined the length of time the play is going to take should be established. Deciding on the amount of time helps to determine which scenes are the most important and need more time to present. It may be determined at this point that some of the scenes are not necessary in order to get the point of the story across. Take out any scenes that are not necessary and refine the play for the specific presentation.

Rehearsing a Play

Before rehearsals begin divide the play into three key parts. This will make it much easier to manage as time progresses. If the play is shorter then it could be divided into two parts (or acts).

1. Setting—What is the best way for students to understand the setting of the play?
   It is important to note that students rely on their personal experiences to interpret what they read. *Jack and the Beanstalk* takes place a long, long time ago. What does that description mean to a student today? It is important to break the setting down into a more

understandable idea. For instance, asking the students about their ideas concerning poor people. What images come to their minds? Direct their attention to the fact that Jack and his mother were very poor and lived a long time ago in a cabin of sorts on the edge of town. After establishing the basic facts of Jack's environment think about what kind of things that Jack and his mother might have in their home. There might be a stove or a table and a cupboard. After brainstorming about the things in Jack's house then have them consider exactly what will be needed to give the impression of all of those things. For instance, a table could be used to establish the idea of a kitchen. Props can also serve to instruct the audience about the location. An example would be a mixing bowl with some kitchen implements on the table. This is a simple example of determining the scene and may be much more involved or even simpler depending on the script. The difference in a live theatrical performance and a movie is the suggestion of location. Live theatre allows the audience to use their imagination in order to fill in the blanks as they watch the story.

2. Points of Action—Determine the things that an audience must see in order to understand the play.

The play *Jack and the Beanstalk* depends on the audience understanding that Jack and his mother are poor. The setting can be relied on to explain this to the audience, but if the setting is merely suggested it becomes difficult. In that case, then the dialogue can be used to instruct the audience on the poverty level of Jack and his mother. It is important that the audience understands what is happening as the story progresses. In addition to the physical setting of the play and the dialogue, it is important that the characters show the feeling of being poor. Jack and his mother should physically reinforce the idea of who they are and what their particular circumstance is. An example of this might be a scene where Jack and his mother are eating a meal. The actions and dialogue should reinforce the idea that they are poor and have very little or even no food to eat. What actions could demonstrate this idea? Perhaps Jack could mention that he is still hungry, or the mother could search for food in the cabinets without success. The original idea for this scene might conjure up grand ideas of a kitchen filled with set pieces and props for the actors to work with. The reality of the available resources in a classroom may limit the availability of props so pantomime might be best. Using pantomime allows the actor to explore areas of the setting that are completed by the imagination of the audience. For instance, if the mother pantomimes searching the cupboards and then sighs and frowns it could easily give the impression that something is wrong.

3. Staging Limitations—Determine if it is feasible to keep each setting due to the physical limitations of the acting space.

An example from *Jack and the Beanstalk* would be the feasibility of showing Jack climbing the beanstalk into the clouds and retrieving the various objects. It would be difficult to construct a beanstalk for the play. An alternative would be to remove the scene where Jack climbs into the sky to visit the giant's palace. In place of this scene another scene could be created that shows Jack after visiting the giant's palace. In this scene, Jack could be explaining to his mother the story of his trek to the palace of the giant while he is showing her the goose and the golden egg. In fact, it is very possible that the majority of this story could be told in two settings, outside Jack's house and the kitchen of Jack's house. Limiting the number of settings makes it much easier to stage a play. Reviewing the play to consider the settings is important to assure the feasibility of presenting the story in the space that is available.

4. Characterization—The traits of the characters should be determine from the beginning. As the play is developed it is important to have a good idea of who each characters are and how they will act within the story. Most characters can be developed in numerous ways so it is important to determine how the characters will be interpreted. The characters of Jack and his mother could be interpreted in several ways. For instance, if Jack is strong and mischievous he would react differently than if he was a quiet, reserved child who created worlds within his own imagination to entertain himself. Consider that Jack's mother is the opposite type of personality such as a strong self-assured woman who control's every aspect of Jack's life. In this scenario, Jack might be unsure of himself and not able to do much on his own. Perhaps, his mother might climb the beanstalk to retrieve the goose and her golden eggs in this portrayal of the story. If the mother climbed the beanstalk it would influence all of the dialogue for the play. Characterization is a key consideration when building the script for the play.

5. Editing—Edit the story for time.
   While creating a play it is important to understand the value of editing the script to make it manageable for the amount of time provided. A fun exercise to help students understand how to condense thoughts. Encouraging student to condense thoughts into a single sentence helps them to understand the importance of editing. The process forces them to prioritize the ideas and scenes within the story. Using *Jack and the Beanstalk* as an example have the students write a summary of the story in ten words or less. The statement, "Jack found magic beans that led him to a fortune" is an example of a sentence that describes the story. Once they have created the ten word statement have them condense it to three words such as "Jack found fortune." Using simple sentences such as these helps demonstrate to students how to approach the editing process.

Creative Dramatics and Children

Children naturally select the most appropriate methods for recreating characters and situations when involved in dramatic play. A key consideration of children when play acting is their reaction to humor. Children express humor in different ways than adults. Many times it takes the form of horseplay and very physical behavior. When a child is so focused on creating or recreating a character in a situation they can become very inwardly focused to an extent that they subconsciously choose the most dramatic actions to portray. Humans have a natural ability to seek out the most dramatic actions in a given situation.

Children's imagination will manifest itself in a very unique manner for each child. The reasoning behind this is that a child's resources for interpretation are very limited. The limitations are based in experiences. If a child has not had a variety of experiences it is difficult for them to imagine something beyond what they have already had the opportunity to synthesize.

Theatre Lingo

Theatre has many terms that are unique. It is important for a teacher to have a working knowledge of basic theatre terms to share with their students.

Action	The characters responses to the given circumstance that drive the story forward.
Antagonist	The character that stands in the way of the protagonist accomplishing their goals.
Apron	The front portion of a stage in front of the curtain.
Arena Theatre	A theatre where the audience sits on all four sides of the stage, or completely surrounds the stage.
Artistic Director	The person in charge of the overall artistic vision of a production.
Backstory	The part of the story that explains what happened to the characters before the story begins.
Blocking	The placement of actors on the stage that determines their movement throughout the play.
Book	In musical theatre the spoken lines of dialogue and the written plot written by the librettist. Does not include the lyrics or music.
Box Office	The ticket office for a theatre
Call	The time the actors are required to be at the theatre.
Choreographer	The person who creates dance movements for a production.
Composer	The person who writes the music for a musical.
Curtain	The start of the show or may actually be a reference to the curtain at the front of the stage.
Dialogue	The spoken text of a play.
Director	The person who turns a written script into a full stage production.
Downstage	The area of the stage closest to the audience.
Flats	The unit pieces that are put together to make a wall for the scenery of a play. They are made of a variety of materials, but traditional they were like an artist's canvas that was stretched tightly over a wooden frame.

House	The area where the audience sits during a performance.
Librettist	The person that writes the book or lines for a musical.
Lyricist	The person who writes the lyrics for a musical.
Lyrics	The sung words of a musical.
Motivation	The conscious or subconscious reason a character chooses to take an action.
Plot	The logical structure of a play.
Property	Sometimes called "props" referring to the small objects that actors handle during a play.
Protagonist	The central character in a play who moves the action of a play forward.

CHAPTER 6
Integrating the Arts

O ne of the most important figures known to creativity is Sir Ken Robinson. Robinson is known internationally for pointing out "If the human mind was restricted to academic intelligence, most of the human culture would not have happened." None of us would want to live in a world without music, dance, theatre, paintings, and architecture. Robinson suggests that these are the "fruits of creativity." "These are rather large factors to leave out of a model of human intelligence."

Hermin/Shutterstock.com

In the book *A Whole New Mind: Why Right Brainers Will Rule the Future* by author Daniel Pink (2006), he states that "how can we better prepare students for great jobs?" Computers are becoming more important all the time, with students only focus on taking test, and getting a satisfactory score. Pink feels as millions do, that to become professionally and personally successful will require risk taking, empathy, and doing innovative thinking. This country was built on creative thinking, and the best way to solve problems is through artistic approaches. The American people are beginning to see that the Fine Arts are very important and necessary for a well developed and well rounded education. The Arts someday may be referred to as the "fourth R."

The Need for the Arts

Why is there a need for the integration of the Fine Arts? The Arts have the capability of changing hearts and minds. People can begin to understand each other in a way that transcends oceans and intellect. The communication between people, which is art based is a symbolic language that exist because all thoughts and ideas cannot be understood only with words.

The contributions for intellect come from the creative problem-solving angle. Seeking connections and synthesizing diverse solutions for modern day issues and problems. Critical thinking is also a part of the contribution. A particular format is used to analyze the details and patterns that are showing up. After doing so, the evidence is compiled and judgments are made and solutions found. Comprehension is understanding and looking for the big ideas or the big picture. Data must be found along with divergent perspectives and then coming up with the important connections. The composition is yet another contribution. The arts offer a vast choice of how to express thoughts feelings or ideas.

Artwork is all around us even on a postage stamp

The social contribution can begin with looking at culture. The arts can look at how people lived or expressed themselves through time. Within a classroom discussion can begin by looking back in history to come up with ideas to make the future better. The arts are great at getting students working together on projects through collaboration. Choirs, large paintings, skits, music making all shape the way students interact and relate to one another. By working together with students they do not know that classrooms become bridges to develop empathy and understanding and create new perspectives teaching one of the most important parts of life; compassion.

Emotional and personal contributions can be made by looking at personal values. Because the arts are something actively participated in they develop intrinsic motivation. There is commitment which gives satisfaction and a curiosity about new ways of thinking. Concentration is improved because the arts demand involvement. Confidence is gained because students learn to take risks and develop courage to try new things. Personal value is enhanced when a student can offer a suggestion that can solve a new problem. Competence and the control of materials and also over mind, body, and voice give new meaning to personal satisfaction.

What Is Integration

The definition of integration comes from the Latin word integare, which means to make whole. It really just means the combining of diverse elements into a whole, where the parts can keep their integrity but the sum of all parts is worth more. What makes our lives full and rich are all the parts added together to make a whole life. Making school more real and life like makes it more interesting. A school day that is spent working to solve individual issues and problems really can become boring for students. If learning can be done where purpose is found along with relevancy then students find meaning.

Usually, the integration has three stages; the first stage is where the teacher will teach with the arts. The teacher will find an art area that they feel they understand and know the best and use it quite often in lesson planning. Sometimes, centers can be set up inside the classroom where students move around using different art model stations. For example, one student might be working on a drawing while another student is writing the lines her character will say in a short play. The second stage that is more meaningful is when teachers have the opportunity to observe different artist such as directors of plays, musicians, painters, etc. In doing so, the teachers feel comfortable asking questions about the best way to plan art into the lesson. Together they come up with ideas that can be best used to reach this particular age child. Again, teachers do usually choose to work in an area that is personally comfortable. Planning is of most importance. If a musical instrument is to be played by the teacher practice is important. Children enjoy singing along as their teacher plays an instrument; however, they are much more impressed by someone who can play as though they have practiced. The third level is where the subject is taught through the arts. The arts are used as learning tools and unit centers. Lessons are taught using an inquiry-based creative problem-solving strategy.

Teaching Practices

Some of the best-teaching practices to integrate the arts are as follows: Art strategies and ideas are used in a way to solve problem by involving the thinking, feeling, and building that changes ideas. Students gain confidence as they learn to become better at singing, speaking, dancing, and drawing. They learn to practice until they reach their individual goal. Students are in classrooms where teachers are enthusiastic about the arts and show confidence in the different areas they teach from. Students understand the how, what, when, and where, of the artistic concepts being taught. Students are given feedback on the work they have done as well as input from peers to improve final project. Students are encouraged to focus more on the process than the end product in the early stages of understanding. The idea of a draft or rough copy without penalty is a good starting point for both the student and the teacher. Teachers slow the learning process down to allow all students to understand concepts and make good judgments.

As students learn more through the integration of the arts, they will have an advantage in the twenty-first century. Problem solver and risk takers will be the leaders of the next generation. This type of thinking does not come from sitting in a desk seven hours a day taking test. This type of leadership comes from the mind of an inquiry based thinker, one who has been developed through the arts.

Art-Focused Thinking

Art-focused thinking can create innovations and how they will best function as they call on visual art, music, theatre, and dance to send a message to the rest of the world. Much learning comes from units designed with hands on learning and problem-solving skills. The world becomes smaller as the "universal language" of man reaches out across the world to offer understanding, ideas, and answers. In order to plan units with an arts focus sometimes, it is best to think of the lessons in a different way.

Travel Planning

When a person decides to travel and visit some far away destination, they generally make plans and think about the different things they will do on this trip. A lesson is exactly the same, in order to facilitate learning a plan must be in place in order to obtain the best experience. Integrated lesson planning begins with the **destination**. The destination is a short phrase that summarizes the objectives for a lesson, or in other words the title of the lesson. The content area represents the **Region** where the trip will take place (math, science, and social studies). When choosing to integrate the arts into a lesson sometimes, one area of the arts is integrated and at other times all three might be integrated. When planning, it is important to think about each individual area of the arts to see if they might be implemented within the lesson. Once the region and destination have been established, then it is time to acquire the **tickets**, or objectives, for the trip. The **packing list** is important in order to plan for the necessary supplies that will be needed to implement the lesson. Having the supplies readily available keeps the lesson flowing and provides for a smooth trip to the destination. The framework or structure of the lesson should be well thought out and **field notes** should be written down in such a way that it is easy to remember how to execute the lesson. The **destination** or purpose of the lesson is the driving force when creating a plan. The tickets (objectives) tie directly to the destination (expected outcomes) of the lesson. When traveling tourists love to collect souvenirs to help them remember the journey. Taking the time to collect **souvenirs** (notes for the future) helps to develop a lesson and improve it each time it is present. An example might be changing a simple approach within the lesson the next time in order to keep the train of thought more tightly focused.

Integrated Lesson Plan

Teacher: **Grade:**

Destination: (title of lesson)

Region: (content area)

Integrated Arts: (circle)   **ART**   **MUSIC**   **THEATRE**

Tickets: (objectives)

Packing List: (supplies)

Field Notes: (framework)

Destination: (expected outcomes)

Souvenirs: (notes for the future)

Yurchenko Yulia/Shutterstock.com

Teaching Objectives

A teacher influences the next generation in a great way. The quality of an education is repre-sented in the societal values and accomplishments of the next generation. It is very important for a teacher to be aware of the impact they are making on this next generation. If students are encouraged to express themselves in a creative and free manner what will that mean for society as a whole in the future? An important thought to consider is that each leader, superstar, and housewife were all in a classroom at one time; however, it is easy to overlook the thought that a hardened criminal or murderer was once in a classroom as well. Consider the students in your classes and what you as a teacher can do to positively influence the lives of your students. The power to change a life is held firmly in the hand of the teacher. A little encouragement today may prevent the mass killing of people in the future.

Elkit/Shutterstock.com

Encourage your students and celebrate their individuality as you carefully craft their individual education. The experiences each student shares create a colorful quilt of memories and knowledge that they will take with them throughout their life's journey.

CHAPTER 7
Appreciating the Arts

Enjoying the arts is possible in a variety of situations. Each situation determines the behavior of the audience during the performance. The advancement of technology has increased the relaxed approach that is taken by many people when experiencing the arts. One hundred years ago going to see a play or hear a symphony was a once in a lifetime event. Audiences took great pride in presenting themselves in their best attire while viewing or listening to the performance. As movie theaters became more common and music was available on phonograph records, the availability of music and theatre was greatly broadened.

As time progressed going to a theatre to view a play or movie was not as convenient as turning on a television set in the living room at home. Music became readily available at home, the office, or even in the automobile through the magic of radio. Progressing even further through the last century, the mass development of technology in the 1960s that occurred as a result of America's desire to go to the moon brought many new devices that could bring the arts to the fingertips of the patron.

Movies were available on video tapes and then compact discs, music went from the phonograph record to the eight track tapes and then cassette tape. The Walkman was invented and music was more portable than ever when the compact disc was introduced to the world of music. Jam boxes allowed the radio, cassette tape, and compact discs to be played on the go. Video rental stores popped up making access to movies just a matter of another item on the list of things to pick up on the way home from work.

The downsizing of the computer created even more opportunities, as laptops were readily available and the world wide web was developed giving access to the arts to anyone that was connected just about anywhere in the world. This technological advancement paved the way for the smart phone and iPad, which gave the owner music in iTunes which allowed them to select a song to listen to at their fingertips. It also created the opportunity to watch videos of movies on demand. The addition of satellite television and radio brings streaming content directly to people anywhere in the world. Allowing access 24 hours a day seven 7 days a week. Theatre, Art, and Music are now available instantly with the swipe or touch of a finger.

Loss of Dignity

Experiencing the arts has historically been a formal affair. In fact, appearing in public at one time meant carefully evaluating one's appearance and taking pride in the choice of apparel. Today, society has become over casual in order to appease the masses and avoid making others feel uncomfortable. This viewpoint fails to consider the fact that dressing up and presenting yourself the best way possible actually shows more respect to other people than by appearing at the local superstore dressed in sweatpants and a tank top that was meant for a slim teenager but instead is bulging at the seams because it is three sizes smaller than it should be. Consider America's crack problem, is it really a good idea to show your underwear in public? Taking a little effort in order to look good at a concert or a play or even at a museum can increase the experience for everyone. The patron will be happy and feel good about themselves and the other patrons will not be offended by the poor choice of clothing. As a teacher it is always good advice to dress for success. Looking professional encourages professional behavior and provides a solid example for the students in the classroom.

Chief Crow Daria/Shutterstock.com

Group Dynamics

When an audience experiences a play or a musical concert, group dynamics come into play. Group dynamics are a common aspect of human existence. Consider family gatherings, community celebrations such as parades, or even a sporting event. Attending a live event is a completely different experience than watching it on television. At a football game, the crowd cheers collectively when the team makes a touchdown, they clap loudly when the band plays the fight song, they also may celebrate with the surrounding people when something exciting happens with "high fives" or other celebratory gestures. This action in the audience is not possible when viewing the game on television since the viewer is not in the crowd. This emotional experience is referred to as group dynamics. Group dynamics provides a heightened emotional experience for the audience. Research has shown that people react much differently in a crowd than they do when experiencing something by themselves.

Experiencing a performance in a crowd causes them to become more emotional and less intellectual due to the reactions of others around them. All humans have an inherent natural desire to fit into a group. Historically, mankind has been associated with tribes and other groups throughout time due to the need for safety and the feeling that safety is more accessible in larger numbers. Hearing other people respond encourages a personal response. The use of a laugh track for television situation comedies demonstrates this idea. The laugh track is played in spots where the writers want to invoke laughter from the audience viewing the show on television. When a viewer hears the audience on the television laughing they tend to respond with laughter. Consider the difference in a television sitcom and a movie comedy. The sitcom is designed to be viewed individually and the movie comedy is meant to be viewed by a crowd. The sitcom uses a laugh track and the movie comedy does not since the crowd will create the responses that are needed to enhance the experience.

Audience Behavior

For thousands of years, the audience sat and watched in a space bathed with light. This changed with Edison's invention of the lightbulb in the late 1850s. The lightbulb allowed light to be manipulated and provide a new sense of focus for the audience who were watching action on a stage. This also allowed a lighting technician to manipulate the lighting levels on the stage and place the audience in total darkness.

Etiquette

The behavior that is desired for a particular occasion is called as etiquette. Enjoying an artistic expression whether it is viewing a painting, listening to a musical performance, or watching a theatrical event demands respect for the artists as well as fellow audience. When visiting an art exhibition, it is not appropriate to yell, scream, or speak in a loud voice. This can be viewed as a distraction and can interfere with the intention of the artist who is presenting their work. Many times soft music will be played as patrons view the various works on display. Although this might seem like an obvious conclusion, children today have not been taught to respect others and the individual right to enjoy a presentation in peace.

Audience etiquette at a musical concert is similar to a live theatrical presentation. Talking among audience members should be limited and take place before the performance, during intermission, or after the performance. An audience at a movie may talk during the movie, but they must do so at the risk of the other patrons taking severe physical action in order to shut them up. Talking removes the audience from the movie and is a complete distraction.

carmen2011/Shutterstock.com

Basic Rules for Audience Members

1. Respect other audience members. Think to yourself, would what I am about to do bother me if I was sitting around me?
2. Cell phones, there is absolutely no reason that a cell phone should interfere with the audience's enjoyment of a performance. Keep your cell phone in silent, or better yet turn it completely off. Consider the performance a vacation from life. Leave your problems at the door and turn your phone off. Do not text, check messages, or use the flashlight in a dark theatre it blinds the people around you.
3. Talking should not take place during a presentation. This does not mean to imply that you are not able to gasp, cry, or laugh in response to the presentation.
4. Coughing is a huge distraction. It would be wonderful to think that coughing could be magically stopped during a performance, but the reality is that would be impossible. Cough drops are a solution, unwrapping them with an extremely loud crinkly wrapper is not a solution. Find cough drops in a tin or already unwrapped in order to save the audience from the crinkly sound of the wrapper during the performance. Try to suppress your coughs if possible.

5. Babies really do not benefit from the arts. Actually, the truth is that they could benefit from exposure to the arts, but the rest of the audience may grow to hate you if the baby is loud and crying. If at all possible make arrangements for the baby to enjoy an excursion away from you for a couple of hours while you as the parent enjoy a few moments without the concerns of caregiving. Parents deserve the opportunity to enjoy a performance without worrying constantly that their child will be a distraction to the audience.

6. Eating should be done at a restaurant not a fine arts performance. The movies have planted the idea that food should be consumed while enjoying the arts. This is not true! Most theatres, galleries, and concert halls do not allow food or drink in the performance venue. Refreshments many times are available in the lobby during intermission.

7. Be a considerate patron. Do not kick the seat in front of you or block the view for an extended period of time of a work of art in a gallery. Try to limit movement throughout the performance in order to lessen the likelihood of distracting others. As a patron you should not steal the focus away from the performers.

8. Leaving during the middle of a performance is incredibly rude!!! Make arrangements to stay until intermission or the end of the performance. Take care of business before taking your seats for the performance. Getting up to leave not only distracts the audience members that you are climbing over in order to exit but also may distract the performers as well.

9. No selfies!!! The playwrights, composers, and artists have worked very hard to bring the artistic expression of their work to you. Although you may relate intimately with the work it does not belong to you. It is a violation of copyright law to take photos, record musical performances, or copy anything from the presentation. Besides the flash can blind the performers and potentially create chaos on the stage.

10. Enjoy the performance. The whole purpose for attending a performance or art exhibit is to have fun and to experience and interpret the art that is being presented.

11. To clap or not to clap, that is the question. The official rule for clapping is really pretty simple. Clapping is appropriate at the end of an Act of a play or at the end of the entire piece of music. Do not clap at the end of a scene or at the end of a movement in a musical piece.

Students and Etiquette

Students rely on teachers to instruct them in proper audience etiquette. A generation has slipped through the school systems without proper training in audience etiquette. As a teacher you have the potential to change the future by modeling and teaching your students appropriate behavior as an audience member. Respect is taught at school, but many times it is not extended to performance etiquette. As your students perform for each other in your classroom, whether it is presenting a report or poem consider it an opportunity to teach them about proper behavior when listening to others. This simple lesson could benefit them for a lifetime.

asejustin/Shutterstock.com